HOW TO PRAY
FOR A FINANCIAL
MIRACLE

HOW TO
PRAY
FOR A FINANCIAL
MIRACLE

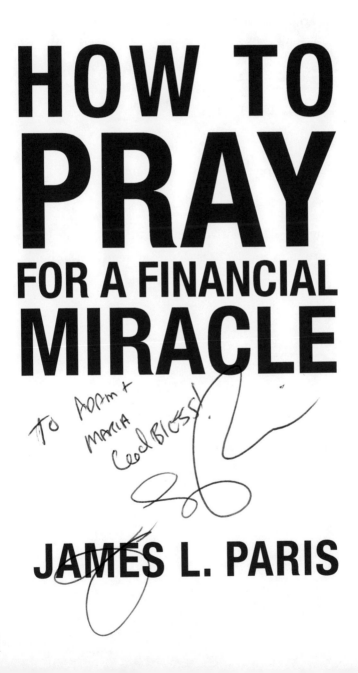

To Adam +
Maria
God Bless!

JAMES L. PARIS

TO DR. RAFAEL PARLADE -

Thank you for being such a great listener and for your countless words of encouragement. You told me that I would be back writing books again and pursuing my life's work. Well, here I am writing another book just like you said. I would not have made it without your kind words and keen insight into my daily struggles. You will never know how much of a difference you made in my life.

CONTENTS

INTRODUCTION

This is a book that I believe I was destined to write. There are some books that are the product of committees and marketing people, but this one landed on the doorstep of my life and I have been preparing to write it for more than a decade.

If you are unfamiliar with my personal story, I went from being a highly successful Christian finance author and owner of a nationwide investment firm, to being dead broke in a matter of about one week. My accountant informed me one morning that my bookkeeper, my own brother, had embezzled nearly two million dollars and that I was completely insolvent. Talk about being hit with a cold bucket of water. So, there I was, a *bankrupt millionaire,* and completely disillusioned about how God could continue to use me in any capacity in the future. Who would listen to my advice if I could not even manage my own financial affairs?

I tried my best to keep things going while I hoped for a way out, but in the end I was unable to recover from the embezzlement. I ended up officially filing for bankruptcy in 2005. In one of the court hearings, the bankruptcy trustee asked me what I did for a living. I was sitting at a table in a courtroom with several dozen individuals that were also going through bankruptcy. I quietly explained that I was a writer and also a money manager. He became very interested and asked in a booming voice, "What was your last book?" and I answered, "Money Management For Those That Don't Have Any." The whole room erupted with laughter. As bad as I felt at that moment, I also laughed. What a perfect title for a financial guy's last book before he ends up in bankruptcy court.

I have to admit that during my good years I built my name and reputation on *looking* the part of a young financial genius. I had multiple country club member-ships, drove expensive cars, lived in expensive homes, wore custom tailored suits, and I enjoyed extravagant vacations around the world. As one person said, I was like the Christian version of Donald Trump. I never really thought of myself at the time as arrogant, but looking back there is no doubt I was. I was the guy that had all of the answers; at least to financial issues. Within a matter of a few days I had no answers, no hope, and believed that my career was over and maybe even my life.

I have struggled over the years wondering if God allowed this all to happen to me, or if it just happened and then he found a way to use it to mold me into a better person. I guess it does not matter which it was.

I can tell you, without a doubt, that my trial by fire changed me. Today I couldn't care less about accumulating money, other than what I need to pay for the basics. I have a totally new perspective; a perspective that places far less value on material wealth than the younger Donald Trump-like Jim Paris. Jim Paris 2.0 can be found on most days wearing a t-shirt and shorts and driving a compact car with more than 100,000 miles on it. I have discovered that God is far more interested in a relationship with me than in how successful I can be as a Christian writer, speaker, and entrepreneur.

During my darkest hours I learned that there were people that loved me *just for me,* and it had nothing to do with my accomplishments or money. This was an amazing discovery! For years I worked so hard to win the approval of people and in the end I learned that I could be loved just for being me.

This book is on prayer, but not any kind of prayer. It is about *how to pray for a financial miracle.* I don't think there is any book like this that you will find anywhere else. There are probably a lot of reasons why. First, many people would dismiss the idea of praying for a financial miracle as greedy, inappropriate, or just downright ungodly. Others might say that God is not in the business of answering financial prayers. I could not disagree more.

Today we are facing the most perilous financial times since the Great Depression. Millions have lost their homes to foreclosure, millions more are without jobs, and according to government statistics American households have lost 40% of their net worth in just the last four years. The street that I live on has multiple empty homes that have been abandoned in foreclosure. I have countless friends, relatives, and acquaintances that are out of work or are working for a fraction of what they used to earn.

While we see our economy collapsing around us, we also see new opportunities. Many of these opportunities are linked to the new economy. For example, a friend of mine went back to school for eighteen months and became a respiratory therapist; he now earns a six figure income and loves his new career. There are countless stories like this that I can share of people finding endless new possibilities working with computers or launching Internet businesses. One new venture that is booming here in Florida is that of cleaning foreclosed homes. People are making more than $500 in a single day simply cleaning out foreclosed properties for the banks. of course, this is an opportunity that is going to be around for several years to come.

Even when times are tough, and they certainly are, there are opportunities if you look for them. Factories are closing in many parts of the country and may never open again, but with that closed door there is at least one new door of opportunity that has opened in another segment of the economy.

Before my financial collapse, my prayer life was minimal, and at times non-existent. It seems like we forget about the Lord when we are enjoying mountaintop successes. He is always there, however, waiting for us to involve Him in our lives again. Sadly, we don't usually seek Him until we are in one of life's valleys. Nonetheless, He is an always faithful friend, ready to step back in and save us when we are in the fiery furnace.

This book is not just about how to pray for a financial miracle, but also what to do after you have finished praying. Your prayer will lead to a plan of action and a journey of faith unlike any other that you have ever experienced. God is just waiting for you right now to start a conversation with Him about your financial challenges. No appointment needed, no special words or magical phrases required, just a humble heart and a receptive spirit and you are on your way to your financial miracle.

CHAPTER ONE

When Your Best Laid Financial Plans Fail

The famed boxer Joe Louis said, "Everyone has a plan until they get hit." Mike Tyson updated the quote by saying, "Everyone has a plan until they get punched in the face." My family's story while I was growing up in Chicago is illustrative of this. My father was a union electrician and got into the trade when he was just fifteen years old, after dropping out of high school. My parents were married when they were only eighteen. They moved into their own home that my dad helped build within a few months of being married. It was the 1960's and dropping out of high school to become an electrician was not as crazy as it would be today. In fact, my dad quickly moved up the ranks and was a 'seasoned veteran,' working as a foreman by his late twenties.

We were not rich, but we had a very good middle class lifestyle. My mother was able to stay home with us as a full time mom. We always took two to three weeks of vacations each year. My dad had all of the toys: boats, RV's, fishing and hunting equipment, you name it. For a blue collar family, we had a very good life and money was not an issue. My grandfather (also an electrician) was largely responsible for getting my dad into the electrician's union and receiving an apprenticeship at such a young age. Because of my grandfather's connections and my dad's work ethic, he seemed to have endless opportunities for work. When one project ended, he quickly found another. He would frequently have opportunities to work overtime, which was almost as good as being able to print your own money. As a member of the union, he would in some cases earn as much as double his regular hourly pay, and on occasion even triple.

Life was good for the Paris family, living in Bridgeview, a quiet southwest suburb of Chicago. That was until 1980. My dad was doing the electrical wiring on a large commercial swimming pool. The pool did not have water in it yet and he was wiring the lights. In order to get into the right position to do this, he had to use a very tall ladder that was put inside the empty pool. Yards away, were large drums of chlorine being prepared to be added to the pool as it would be filled with water after my dad finished the wiring. My dad became dizzy from the overwhelming amount of chlorine in the air, lost his balance, and fell more than 20 feet, landing flat on his back.

I was a freshman in high school and remember coming home that day on the bus. I was greeted by a neighbor who explained to me that my dad had been hurt at work and that my mother was with him at the hospital. I was reassured that everything would be OK, but that day would change my father's life and our family's forever.

My dad had broken his back and would face years of hit and miss surgeries that simply did not come close to resolving the chronic pain he was dealing with. Ultimately, a metal rod was surgically inserted in his back to replace the broken vertebrae. One complication led to the next, and he simply could not live with the pain. Each surgery brought with it renewed hope that his pain would go away and he could get back to a normal life. In most cases, our high hopes were dashed and things would not improve much, if at all, for him. It would be more than ten years before his medical condition would stabilize. Despite ultimately finding a way to manage the pain, my dad never was able to return to work, becoming permanently disabled, and left the workforce at the age of just thirty four.

Being a member of the union, he had great benefits, or so we thought. After receiving about nine months of disability income, without warning, the insurance company cut us off. Tension around our home was already high with my dad's medical situation. Now, there would be no money coming in. Absolutely nothing.

As much as my dad was an excellent provider and a hard worker, he was not one to save money. Like many blue collar families, all the bills were paid but there was not a lot of money in the bank. What I am about to share with you is the real inspiration for this book. You see, for several years our family lived on daily financial miracles. The insurance company cut us off, but God continued to provide. While my parents engaged an attorney to pursue his disability claim in court, we were literally supported by one financial miracle after the next.

It was traumatic enough for me as a young teenage boy to see my dad in such a state, but even worse to come to grips with our family's financial circumstances. Most kids don't really think much about where the money comes from for the utility bills, food, clothing, medical care, gas, etc. All of the things you need are simply there for you and you take them for granted.

The bedroom that I shared with my brother (who was six years younger) was directly off the kitchen in our suburban home. In fact, the room was once a formal 'dining room' that was later enclosed and turned into a bedroom after my brother was born. There were long stretches of time that I would not see my mom all that much during those years. I would come home from school and there would be no one waiting for me. It was just me, my brother, and my sister. When my dad was in the hospital my mom basically lived there, trying to do whatever she could to make sure he was getting good medical care. She would leave very early in the morning and then come home about eight or nine in the evening.

I remember my mom's typical routine of coming in at about 8 pm and then making the rounds to check on the three of us. She would ask if we had dinner, usually comment about the house being dirty, ask us if we needed anything for the next day of school, etc. She would then begin returning phone calls using the kitchen phone. Our family had hundreds of people praying for us and wanting the latest news on my dad's prognosis. My mom would sometimes talk on the phone for two or three hours while sitting at the kitchen table. The wall between the kitchen and my bedroom was paper thin and although she probably did not realize it, I heard every word.

I remember hearing how bad off my dad was physically, that he had gone into a deep depression over his circumstances, and most off all, how we had no money.

People would ask, and my mother was very open about the fact that we were dead broke. I remember being so upset about all of this that I would cover my head with as many pillows as I could find trying to block out what I was hearing. With each new phone call, I would hear the same story over and over again. I remember many nights quietly crying under all those pillows so that my mother could not hear me. Many of those nights the last thing I remembered was crying and then waking up the next morning.

I knew that at the age of fourteen there was not much I could really do, but I began working at a local Italian restaurant after school and on the weekends. I had several such jobs while in high school. While I did not earn enough money to really make any difference in my family's circumstances, I was able to at least begin supporting myself. I bought my own clothes, car, got most of my meals for free at my various restaurant jobs, and contributed toward groceries for the house. I really liked working and staying busy, and it made me feel good that at least I was not a burden in any way financially for my parents. My favorite job of all was working for White Castle. Since it was a 24 hour operation, I signed up for the 11 pm to 7 am shifts on Friday and Saturday nights. This allowed me to participate in all of my marching band activities and still land a decent paycheck each week. I also got free White Castle hamburgers, which to a hungry teenager was quite a fringe benefit. I am sure when I left to go off to college that their profits spiked when they no longer had the expense of feeding me.

I don't exaggerate when I tell you that there were daily financial miracles at our home. I cannot even remember how many times people would drive up and unload hundreds of dollars of groceries from their cars into our refrigerator and cabinets. This happened over and over again. We received money always just before a critical bill needed to be paid. I remember one time when my mom was very worried about some upcoming financial deadlines, she went out to the mailbox and there was a sizable money order simply signed "A. Friend" for just the amount we needed.

For more than four years our family was literally supported by manna from heaven. I know my parents tapped our home equity and also a cash value life insurance policy they had, but for the most part we were being supported by fellow Christians that simply loved us and knew that we had a financial need.

My parents were so impacted by that experience that they became lifelong givers. They just loved helping people in need. They knew first hand what it was like to have nothing and how wonderful it was when people were so generous to give sacrificially meeting *their* needs. My parents love to give was taken to new levels when several years ago they took over leadership of a food pantry ministry at Apopka Assembly of God (just outside of Orlando, FL). For nearly a decade they have donated their full time efforts gathering food from local merchants and feeding on average 200 families a week. If you want a glimpse into this ministry, you can watch a short video at *www.orlandofoodministry.org*. My father went to be with the Lord in September of 2011, but my mom continues leading the Storehouse ministry at Apopka Assembly.

There were quite a lot of lessons I learned from those four years our family struggled. First, I learned that God is faithful and is ready, willing, and able to meet our needs. I also learned from my mother that there is no shame in sharing your needs with God's people. When I went through my own financial collapse I told no one. In the beginning I would lie before I would admit I was struggling, and that was not productive for me or those that would have loved to help.

In many ways I was a lot like my own father. I was married at the young age of twenty one and was bound and determined to make a success of myself. Going through those fours years in Chicago with my family was an incredible motivation for me to take whatever measures I could to never end up in need. The critical point that I was missing was that I was placing all of my confidence and trust in my *own plan*. If I could just accumulate enough money, corporations, streams of income, I would never go through a financial valley again. It became my life's passion and pursuit.

By the age of thirty I was on top of the world financially. I had written numerous books, had my own radio and television shows and several income producing businesses. We expanded our operation to three locations, two in Florida and an office in Dallas, TX. In one year alone, I was a guest on The 700 Club more than 20 times. Despite my 'success' and great plan I still ended up dead broke when my bookkeeper, my own brother, embezzled nearly two million dollars from the businesses.

I want to share with you a blog post I wrote a few years ago, inspired by my own confusion about success -

WHO'S REALLY IN CONTROL OF OUR FINANCIAL SUCCESS?

"We know that in everything God works for good with those who love him, who are called according to his purpose."
–Romans 8:28 (RSV)

I recently viewed a video of a motivational speaker addressing a gathering of ten thousand people. The man truly had an amazing story of success, in spite of grave personal adversity and offered a truly inspiring message. When listening to such an invigorating speaker, we all might tend to accept everything he says as sensible, after all this guy is "successful" and who are we to question his philosophies of success, right?

His opening line was one that is employed by many success-oriented speakers: "You are where you're at in your life because of decisions you have made. The level of success you have achieved is simply a compilation of all of your decisions and actions up to this point in your life." The speaker went on to say, "No one ever becomes a success if they cannot first take responsibility for their current circumstances." This kind of statement is certainly an enigma and a tough one to come to grips with as a Christian. I thought for a moment, could he be right? Can we all just sit down and make a list of our life's decisions and accompanying actions and determine that we have steered ourselves to our present destination? Are we truly just the "captain of our own ship?" How does God fit into all of this?

"I never blame myself when I'm not hitting. I just blame the bat, and if it keeps up, I change

bats. After all, if I know it isn't my fault that I'm
not hitting, how can I get mad at myself?"
–YOGI BERRA

Throughout my career I have counseled hundreds, and through my seminars and other public appearances, tens of thousands. While it is clear that many of those seeking my financial advice had made bad decisions and seemed to me to be at least partly responsible for their financial predicament, many *truly were victims*. The stories would fill volumes: people who were facing financial loss due to actions of a business partner, spouse, natural or economic disaster, the economy, unexpected health problems; the list is endless.

How do we deal with the reality that no matter what we do or what plans we make, in the end we cannot control the final outcome? Show me a motivational speaker who uses that as an opening thought and I will show you 10,000 empty seats. How do we come to grips with the reality that *even our best laid plans can and do fail?* How can we look at all of the broken pieces of our lives and not feel guilty and hopeless?

Regardless of the reason our finances may be failing, God offers us a new perspective on life's challenges. He promises to those who love him an amazing gift. The gift is a new tomorrow, a renewed life, and that he will take our financial tragedy and create something even better than what we could have hoped for in our own "success plan."

What an unsettling thought that we are not ultimately in control of our own lives. It is, for most people, painfully obvious what *they have done to contribute to their own failure.* It is also our responsibility to strive each day to make the *most of the material blessings that God has provided to us.* In the end, *we cannot control the final outcome.* Accepting this truth is a bold step, but realizing that our Heavenly Father can turn our failures into success provides the ultimate peace and security and true "success."

CONCLUSION

I don't care what plan you come up with, there is no guarantee that you will financially succeed. Wealth is fleeting. You may be in a good financial position today, but none of us knows what tomorrow holds. This was the biggest lesson that I learned going through my own financial collapse.

> *"Therefore everyone who hears these words of mine and puts them into practice is like a wise man who built his house on the rock. The rain came down, the streams rose, and the winds blew and beat against that house; yet it did not fall, because it had its foundation on the rock. But*

everyone who hears these words of mine and does
not put them into practice is like a foolish man
who built his house on sand. The rain came down,
the streams rose, and the winds blew and beat
against that house, and it fell with a great crash."
–MATTHEW 7:24-27 (NIV)

Every time I read this verse it seems directed at me personally. I had, in the world's terms, built quite a secure future for myself. I did not know it at the time, but I was building my house on sand. The only thing that lasts forever is our relationship with the Lord. He is our rock.

CHAPTER TWO

Wrestling With The Concept Of Prayer

There have been thousands of books written on the topic of prayer, but, to my knowledge, none dedicated entirely on how to pray for a financial miracle. From what I understand, as a category, books on prayer represent an extremely popular niche within Christian publishing. One man told me, "If you want to sell a lot of books in the Christian market, write one on prayer." I guess I will have to wait to see what the sales figures are to find out if he was right. What is it about the concept of prayer that seems so elusive that we spend our lives searching for an understanding of it?

Like many people, I have struggled with understanding the mystery of prayer since I was a young boy. Talk to ten Christians and you will likely get ten different perspectives on prayer. To illustrate my own confusion, let me relate my own personal story of two prayers.

At the age of five, in a childhood accident, I ran through a plate glass window in the storm door of our family home in suburban Chicago. This was a parent's worst nightmare: the sound of breaking glass, the screams of my friends, and blood everywhere. My mother came running down the stairs of our two story home and there I was completely covered in blood. To make matters worse, my dad (who was a part time volunteer fireman), was not home but at the firehouse. This was before the days of dialing 911, but whatever the number was to call she dialed it and a legion of firemen and rescue vehicles appeared within about five minutes. I remember my mother crying uncontrollably, and despite being covered with blood, I felt like I should be doing something for *her* and had little concern about my own circumstances.

I must have been in shock because I honestly did not feel any pain. There was plenty of blood pouring out from multiple areas of my face and neck, but I don't remember being upset about anything except my mother's hysteria.

Before I knew what was happening, I was being placed on a stretcher and loaded into an ambulance. I remember my dad riding in the ambulance with me. I vividly recall various emergency workers reassuring me as they applied pressure and bandages to my multiple wounds. I remember, ignoring my wounds, that it was quite exciting to get a real ride in an ambulance (with sirens and lights and everything). I guess this provides a keen insight into the mind of a five year old, as I had no idea what that day would mean to the *rest* of my life.

My parents prayed and prayed and everyone that we knew prayed for me. I sincerely believe those prayers likely saved my life, but as a result of the accident I became permanently blind in my left eye. The doctors said that I had also nicked my jugular vein, and had the glass gone even the tiniest bit further I would have likely bled to death. I still have noticeable scars on my face, hands, and arms from that day.

Not only did my parents pray, they enlisted whatever advice they could get from any and every source they knew. I remember one very well meaning relative that determined that my retina could reattach and my sight be restored if I only took enough vitamins and supplements. For months I was forced to take huge vitamin pills. Some days I had to take a dozen or more of them. Everyone was praying for 'Little Jimmy' (as I was known), and I mean everyone.

Months and months went by and the prayers, vitamins, trips to the best eye doctors in Chicago, and I was still unable to see in my left eye. My mother, years later, described my father's reaction to this as a total emotional collapse. She said he fell on his bed and cried for hours the night of my accident. My dad was a tough guy and I was very surprised to learn about this years later when my mother decided to share it with me.

It took a long time for my dad to finally give up hope on my medical prognosis. I grew up for years with a very damaged and blind left eye. My eye would noticeably drift and would rarely move in tandem with my right eye. The blind eye also began to develop cataracts. As a result of the continuing degradation of my blind eye, my good eye was beginning to be affected. The doctors recommended repeatedly that my eye be surgically removed and that I get a prosthesis. My dad would just not accept this. He believed that continued prayer and advances in medical technology would at some point bring my sight back.

At the age of eighteen, with no other viable options, my left eye was surgically removed and I now have a prosthetic eye. This surgery resolved so many issues for me and I actually looked 'normal' for the first time since the accident. The blind eye got smaller and atrophied over the years to the point that it was noticeable from a considerable distance. The prosthetic eye looked great and all of my apprehension about it quickly dissipated. I live today with this 'handicap' and do just fine. I am a black belt practitioner of Tae Kwon Do, an avid sailor, and participate in all kinds of outdoor activities.

Nonetheless, despite years and years of prayers, my parents wishes for my left eye to be healed did not come to fruition.

MY SECOND EYE INJURY

If you didn't think this whole ordeal was more than enough for my parents to deal with, we move on to my second eye injury which occurred when I was nine years old (just four years later). Since I could only see in one eye, I was fitted with black, horn-rimmed glasses. These were not just any old pair of glasses, but special safety glasses with lenses that were considered to be bulletproof. My dad spared no expense to make sure that my one remaining eye was protected. I was not allowed to go anywhere without those glasses, especially when I was playing sports.

It was a cool Saturday afternoon and a bunch of us guys pulled together a five on five street hockey game. The game would take place in my own driveway, which had recently been upgraded from gravel to blacktop. I remember the game going about an hour before one of my good friends, Matthew Payton, was headed toward our goal and was setting up a slap shot. I decided to get in front of him and the shot, and I stood my ground as he approached. At a distance of about two feet he pulled his stick back as I moved toward him in an effort to stop him from scoring. The next thing I remember is laying flat on the ground, looking up, and seeing my friends standing over me screaming.

Yes, another bloody scene and my mother was again home alone. The lenses of the safety glasses I was wearing shattered into tiny pieces that went into my good eye. There was not quite as much blood this time, but it did not take long for my mom to come running outside. The emergency call was made, and an army of firemen arrived. My dad was working at his regular job as an electrician and it took him about an hour to get to the hospital from his work site. My mom was beside herself and it did not take long for her to begin considering what this might mean. Would her son be completely blind? What were the odds that a kid could have two separate accidents like this and then end up in such a situation? How could the safety glasses have shattered as they did? Wasn't this the exact kind of circumstance that these glasses were designed to prevent?

After being patched up at the emergency room we were to meet an eye specialist at his office. Despite it being a Saturday night, the office was opened up just for us due to the critical nature of the situation. After being examined for about an hour, I was moved to a chair in the lobby. I guess it was one of those moments where the parents would be hearing the harsh truth of their child's diagnosis, and it was better if I was not not in the room with them. For several minutes I heard the doctor talking, but could not really make out what he was saying. I began to hear my mother crying uncontrollably. I knew this could not be good news, but honestly I was still in a daze after the whirlwind day it had been.

I later learned that the doctor informed my parents that there was nothing he could do for me. The eye was patched up and only time would tell how things would come out. He did tell them there was a chance I could end up completely blind. He then said a very odd thing (not what you might expect in a medical office). He asked my mom if she believed in God. My mother said that she absolutely did. "You need to pray to your god, keep your son in bed, and bring him back to my office on Monday morning." I was taken home directly to bed with a large patch over my eye. I was not allowed to get up except to use the bathroom. I can tell you that I could not help but to pull the eye patch back enough to peek out to get a sense of whether I could see or not. I remember seeing nothing but a blur, as if I was under water. I was only nine but this really did begin to scare me. Was I going to end up completely blind?

The next day was Sunday and I was kept home from church that morning, still ordered to stay flat in bed. Our Pastor, Albert Andreasen, insisted that my parents bring me to church that Sunday night. He said that there would be a special healing service just for me. My mom tried to explain to the pastor that I was not allowed to be moved from my bed, but he was relentless in insisting that I be brought to church that night to be prayed for.

I remember being led step by step into church that night, eye patch and all. We grew up just four doors down the street from my Uncle Terry and Aunt Ellen and my six cousins. Although they were Baptists, they all came to this charismatic healing service at the First Assembly of God Church in Joliet, IL. At the appointed moment, after the praise and worship segment of the service, I was brought to the front of the church. The pastor annointed me with oil and began to pray for me. I felt the presence of God like I had never felt in my life before. It was like being dipped into a tub of warm water. I felt a sense of electricity running through my entire body. It was an experience I will never forget.

One of my cousins, Tony Paris, was described by my mother as having been especially moved while praying for me. Tony was just ten years old at the time. I remember my mom commenting on the drive home how she could not believe how fervently Tony was praying for me. I understand that tears were streaming down his face and he had his hands lifted toward heaven. This may give you a snapshot of the scene that took place at the altar of that church as dozens of people of all ages surrounded me praying for my healing.

The next day (Monday morning), we were the first appointment of the day at the eye specialist's office (yes, the same guy that suggested that my mom "pray to her god"). He sat me down on a stool and removed the eye patch. I remember being able to see so clearly and I was stunned how that could be. The blurriness was gone completely. The doctor just stared at me with an extremely puzzled look on his face. He then began to examine my eye with a scope. After a few minutes he turned to my mother and said, "I can't explain it but this is not the same eye I saw on Saturday night." My mom was completely confused at this point and asked him to clarify what he was saying. He responded, "There is nothing wrong with this eye, what did you do?" My mom shared with him about the special healing service we had the night before. He said, "Well, I can't explain it but the eye is completely normal; even the cuts are gone."

My mother was still unable to come to grips with what had just happened and asked him what the next step was, when we would be coming back to his office, etc. He said, "Ma'am you are not understanding me. Take your boy home there is nothing wrong with his eye." I can tell you that I heard all of this first hand and at the age of nine was completely confused about what this all meant. The patch was taken off and I was able to see perfectly. In fact, my sight was even <u>better</u> than before the accident. To this day, I have unusually good sight in my one eye. I have been able to participate in a wide range of sports and outdoor activities. There is no doubt I was healed, but in the process I also believe that God actually gave me better sight in my right eye than I even had before the accident.

I still struggled for years dealing with the numerous issues related to the blindness in my left eye. While I was grateful for my healing, I frequently wondered why God would heal one eye and not the other. I don't really have an answer to this question. We know from scripture that there are occasions where physical ailments stick with people despite their most sincere prayers. In 2 Cor. 12:7-10 we read about the Apostle Paul's thorn in the flesh. While we don't know what his affliction was, we know that he lived with it despite being blessed by untold numbers of miracles, including the Acts 9 account of Jesus speaking to him as a bright light bursted from the heavens. The Apostle Paul, credited with authoring more books of the New Testament than any other writer, wanted us to know that he simply had a physical ailment he had to live with. I believe this is significant. Our prayers do not always lead to the outcome that we want.

HOW DOES THIS RELATE TO YOUR FINANCIAL PRAYERS?

I have heard some people cleverly say that God always *answers* our prayers, but sometimes the answer is *no*. Personally, I have always disliked that way of explaining so called *unanswered prayer*. It seems like an extreme oversimplification and portrays God as being as random as a Magic 8 Ball. I am sure you would not have picked up this book unless you were going through a serious financial valley. If you are a Christian, no doubt you have already prayed for a solution to your problem. I guess it would also be fair to assume that you are still struggling with at least one or more major financial challenges or you would likely not be reading this book.

WHY WE DON'T ALWAYS GET THE RESULTS WE SEEK IN PRAYER

To go back to the 'sometimes God says no' explanation, I do believe there is some truth in this. Imagine being on a journey and ending up lost. You approach a large raging river. You begin to pray for God to give you a way to be able to cross the river, since you believe this is the only way you can be rescued. Maybe if you keep praying long and hard enough, He will lead you to a shallow spot in the river that will allow you to cross. Maybe He will reveal to you an area with several large boulders that you can use to leap frog your way to the other side. Even better: He will guide you to a beautiful bridge that you can simply walk over. A close second; someone will pull up on shore with a boat and offer to transport you to the other side. You fervently pray and you imagine these various scenarios. Perhaps you even envision God giving you wings and temporarily granting you the ability to fly across the river. You are 100% sincere; you have faith that God can answer your prayer in any of these ways, or even in some manner you have not even considered yet.

After days of waiting for God to provide you with a means to get across the raging river, you finally give up. "I guess God is just not hearing my prayers," you think to yourself. You begin looking for another way. You are surprised to discover a road not very far at all from where you have spent days hoping and praying for a way across the river. You begin to walk down the road and within a few minutes, through a break in the tree line, you see a small town. You realize that you will soon be rescued!

I cannot tell you how many times I have metaphorically been in this exact set of circumstances. No, not an actual raging river, but some impossibly large problem that I needed to resolve. I would first come up with my own direction and then go to God with my plan. I would pray that He would bring the plan together just as I had devised it. I hope you are starting to smile a little while reading this. Don't you see how ridiculous we can all be in how we approach God in prayer? But, this is what many of us do. We are not praying for God's will but for Him to fulfill *our* own plan.

WHY WE BELIEVE OUR PRAYERS ARE 'UNANSWERED'

It is true that in many cases we have to simply trust that the Lord knows what is best for us. This is very easy to write but not easy to put into practice. I can't think of a good reason why God chose to restore the sight in my right eye but not my left. Maybe it was to provide me with this life lesson to share with you through this book. My mom often quotes the well worn phrase, "God works in mysterious ways." There are times when we pray and we simply have to trust that our Heavenly Father is working a greater plan than our own. I have shared my story many times with individuals that have prayed for a physical healing and did not receive it. If we understand that, in the end, our ultimate healing will come when we are given a new body in heaven, this may all make a lot more sense to us today.

HOW DID JESUS PRAY?

I can think of no more amazing prayer than that of Jesus praying in the Garden of Gethsemane the night before his crucifixion:

> They went to a place called Gethsemane, and Jesus said to his disciples, "Sit here while I pray." He took Peter, James and John along with him, and he began to be deeply distressed and troubled. "My soul is overwhelmed with sorrow to the point of death," he said to them. "Stay here and keep watch." Going a little farther, he fell to the ground and prayed that if possible the hour might pass from him. "Abba, Father," he said, "everything is possible for you. Take this cup from me. Yet not what I will, but what you will."
> –MARK 14:32-42 (NIV)

I still cry today every time I read this passage. Here is Jesus Christ, the Son of God, praying for deliverance from His imminent crucifixion, but accepts God's will, knowing that in just hours He will face the most painful execution known to the ancient world.

GOD'S WILL – WHAT IS IT?

We hear the phrase "God's will" so often, but do we really know what it is? I feel that many times when I hear Christians make reference to God's will it is done so as if it is the plague. How often have you heard fellow

Christians say things like, "I would really love for God to provide a solution to my problem, but I guess I can accept His will in the matter." A verse that I have learned to live by is **Psalm 37:4 (NIV) "Delight yourself in the Lord and He will give you the desires of your heart."** I have heard many sermons preached on this verse and there is a lot to absorb if you just sit back and think about it for a few minutes. What I take away from this verse is that if I am in a proper relationship with the Lord, my desires will be His desires for me. God and I are on the same page, and the struggle between what I want and what God has planned for me disappears. I can also trust him that my 'unanswered prayers' are part of an even better plan for me than I can conceive on my own.

The reality is that here on earth, I doubt we ever reach that point of being in perfect harmony with the Lord, or completely understanding His plans for our lives. I do believe, however, that as we draw closer to Him our desires do change. One thing that is amazing about prayer is that prayer changes you! You may still be facing the same financial mountain, but a new perspective gained through prayer makes it an easy climb. Does this mean that we reach a point where we are happy to accept the outcome of things, no matter what they may be? Realistically no, but I believe there is a partial answer here to the mystery of prayer.

HOW DOES THIS RELATE TO MY PERSONAL FINANCES?

In chapter five, I will share with you a method of prayer that has been life-changing for me. I believe that God revealed this method of prayer to me, not just to keep to myself but to share with you, as well.

CHAPTER THREE

A Financial Miracle At A Jazz Festival

I began playing the trumpet in the fourth grade. After going to college for music, I ended up on the road touring full time as a musician. In fact, that is how I met my wife Ann. Ann was a singer in one of the Christian music groups I toured with in the 1980's. After my financial collapse in 2002, I really hit an emotional low. I don't know if the word depression would be sufficient to describe my mental state. My wife suggested that it would be good therapy for me to start playing the trumpet again.

It had been seventeen years since I had really played and I wondered if I still had the ability to do so. It was really the best thing I could have done at the time. I started playing again and immediately found a seat in a local seventeen piece big band called the Moonlighters (the name aptly makes clear that we all have day jobs). I finally had something to be excited about, despite my financial world collapsing around me. I started practicing every day and looked forward to Thursday nights when the band would rehearse. This band has become a family to me. I have met so many wonderful people by being involved in this group over the last ten years. Most of the band members are retired and had varied careers ranging from a Navy Admiral to engineers to school music teachers. The group's current director, Dr. Joe Mirante, is an ear, nose, and throat doctor in Ormond Beach, FL. The original founder was John Feulner, a wonderful Christian man that went to be with the Lord three years ago. I still play first trumpet in this band and consider our Thursday night rehearsals the high point of my week.

My son, Jimmy, is also a trumpet player. I suggested he select the trumpet years earlier when he joined the grade school band. Now that I was playing again, Jimmy got to come with me on some of my professional gigs and watch me playing with the big band. One night I actually got the guys to let him sit in with us for the last number of the show. There he was, about twelve years old, sitting up on the bandstand playing the fourth trumpet part with sixteen other professional musicians. It was the equivalent of a Little League baseball player getting to take the field with the Chicago White Sox. He was thrilled and so was I.

Once my son Jimmy reached high school age, he became a regular member of the band. He did not even have his driver's license yet but he was playing with a professional music group. One summer he desperately wanted to attend the University of North Florida Jazz camp in Jacksonville. The tuition was nearly $900. I was in no position to pay the entire amount for him. I was able to come up with half. We drafted a short letter and made seventeen copies of it and passed it out at the next band rehearsal. The letter simply said that Jimmy wanted to attend the jazz camp and that he was short about $450 to be able to go. We included the official name of the camp so that those donating by check could make their checks payable directly. At the next rehearsal, Jimmy received several envelopes from the guys in the band. After we got home and opened them up, we had received exactly what was needed for him to go!

I will never forget, weeks later when we dropped him off at UNF for the camp how several workers during the registration process commented, "You are the kid who had his tuition paid by several different people, right?" It was a great reminder that he was not there only because of Ann and I but through the kindness of my musical brothers. The Lord provided me with an opportunity to begin playing the trumpet again and not only that, with a wonderful new family of fellow musicians that truly loved me and my son. Yes, another financial miracle and there would be many more to come.

TRANSITIONING FROM CHRISTIAN FINANCIAL GUY BACK TO PRO TRUMPET PLAYER

As the months progressed I ended up being invited to play in a second big band. While playing with this band I met a saxophone player from Palm Coast named Paul Ricci. Paul and I started a two piece combo called '2 *Guys With Horns'* and began performing in night clubs all over Daytona Beach and St. Augustine. It was surreal thinking about how just a few years earlier I was Jim Paris the financial guy and now I was being paid to play my trumpet several nights a week.

I was still financially broker than broke. Even though I was getting paid on my trumpet gigs it was not much, and it was definitely not enough to replace the income that I lost when my companies closed after the embezzlement.

My son and I also began to find as many opportunities as possible to go and listen to live jazz. Money was limited, so when the words 'free' and 'jazz' were discovered in the local newspaper event calendar we took notice. In 2008 the small beach side town where I live hosted a jazz festival. It was a little confusing as there were multiple venues throughout the city where the performances would be. Some of the performances were free and others were very pricey.

It was a Sunday and we went to one of the venues, which is a shopping village that also has a small hotel connected to it. In the center of the open air plaza is a large stage that some of the bands would be performing on. We were especially interested in hearing the famed trumpet player Eddie Henderson, a jazz legend and the head of the jazz program at The Julliard School of Music in New York.

We were hoping and praying that his performance was going to be one of the free ones at the shopping village, but we were wrong. What happened next still brings tears to my eyes today. We were walking around the shopping village asking if anyone knew where Eddie Henderson would be performing, as his show time was within an hour. We finally found someone that had the answer. He told us that Henderson was playing on the stage at the high school about three miles away. I found out at that in order to attend that performance it would have cost $125 for Jimmy and I to get tickets.

I told Jimmy that we could not to go to the concert and he was a real trooper and completely understood. Our kids learned during those years that there were a lot of things we just could not afford and they never made an issue of it with Ann or I. As we were walking out to our car we passed by the lobby of the small hotel. Walking down the steps into the lobby was a man carrying a trumpet case. I walked into the lobby to see who it was and I was shocked that I thought it might be Eddie Henderson. Of course, when you meet someone famous in person there is always that moment when you second guess yourself. I sheepishly asked, "Are you Eddie Henderson?" He said, "Yes, I am. Are you a trumpet player?" I asked, "How did you know?" He replied, "I can see the scar." (Most of us trumpet players can spot each other from across the room since we all have the telltale physical signs of what years of pressing a metal mouthpiece up against your lips will do).

Henderson said, "Are you coming to my show?" I did not know what to say, I was frozen for a minute. There I was standing with Eddie Henderson face to face and I had no money to buy tickets to his show. I looked down at my son, who was completely stunned that we were standing there with Eddie Henderson, and then I regained eye contact with him. I explained that we would love to see his show but I was going through some hard times financially and could not afford the tickets. I was not expecting anything from him but felt that I needed to give him an ample excuse about why we were not able to go.

Without even one second of hesitation he said, "You are going as my guest." Just as he said that a white limousine pulled up to the front door of the hotel. I was still standing there frozen in place unable to move or speak. Henderson said, "Come on, get in, let's go; you can ride with me." I looked down at my son and his face was beaming with a smile from ear to ear. Not only were we being invited to go to the concert for free, but we would be riding in the white stretch limousine with Eddie Henderson! This was simply unbelievable.

We rode with Eddie to the concert venue across town. We got out of the limousine with him and began to walk to the entrance. Eddie was greeted by the top brass of the jazz festival, but we were stopped at the door. The ticket taker asked us for our tickets. My heart sank for a moment, and then Eddie turned to them and said, "These are my guests." At that point we were waived through and allowed to pick any seat we wanted in the theater.

My son and I were in awe during the concert as Henderson played his signature tunes like 'Someday My Prince Will Come." I was just so grateful to be able to be there. It was like we had won a contest. I later wrote a letter to the president of Julliard sharing with him this act of kindness on the part of Professor Henderson.

I almost forgot that we had left our car about three miles across town back at the shopping village. Eddie did not forget. He came out after his show and found us and said, "You need a ride back, don't you?" We rode back with him in the limo to the hotel at the shopping village. I probably thanked him a hundred times I was so grateful.

Some may consider this just a coincidence, but I know it was a miracle. That day the Lord looked down and saw a father and son that wanted to attend a jazz concert but did not have the money to do so. Imagine the odds that I would walk past the hotel at just the moment that Eddie Henderson was coming into the lobby? I did not even know he was staying at this hotel, or even for sure, where, or exactly when he was playing.

The way we were greeted was if he was expecting us. I can tell you this was a truly remarkable day that my son and I will never forget. I still get chills today when I think about how this all happened. There is no doubt that the Lord had arranged it all.

CHAPTER FOUR

Becoming A Bankrupt Millionaire

My financial collapse began in 2002. This was very hard to take in so many ways, but mostly since it involved my brother. My brother and I were so close (or at least I thought). After we were each married and had our own families, we celebrated virtually every holiday together. Every time one of our kids had a birthday there was a big party at one of our homes. Christmas, Easter, Thanksgiving, Fourth of July, there was always a gathering. As mentioned in the introduction, I was devastated to learn from our auditor that my brother had been embezzling from my businesses for several years.

As I began to close down my corporations and hand out final paychecks to employees, it seemed surreal. How could this have happened? Why did I not see it? The embezzlement not only got by me but also our outside accounting firm that performed our annual audits. This collapse had a domino effect on just about every part of my life. There were so many problems that I had to face and there was little time to begin dealing with them.

THE AMAZING SUPPORT OF MY LOVING WIFE

My wife and I met when we were both musicians in a Christian music group. I was twenty one and Ann was 26. There were ten people in the group, I played trumpet and Ann was a singer and dancer. It was sort of like a show you would see at Disney. We were really just friends in the beginning. There were some performance contracts that gave us a lot of down time. Ann and I would usually end up together going to a movie or a shopping mall. I think she thought of me as a younger brother. The age difference made us consider anything more than a friendship as unrealistic, so we were both just having fun as friends and we were happy in our comfort zones.

Well, you already know the ending to the story. Ann and I began a romance that has lasted now for more than twenty seven years. Last year we celebrated our twenty fifth wedding anniversary. What I am about to share with you was the most difficult part of this book to write. Ann stood by me during the darkest period of my life. I remember sharing my story with a lady who commented that my wife must be a real angel to have stuck by me. That is so true, Ann was always there and never blamed me or offered anything other than encouraging words through it all.

Here is a blog post that I wrote on my twenty fifth wedding anniversary -

"There is no doubt that meeting Ann was an integral part of God's plan for my life and she has been the most amazing wife to me and mother to our children. Ann and I met twenty seven years ago when we were both touring as professional musicians. She was a singer and dancer and I was a trumpet player. We would never have been paired up on eHarmony and there were plenty of reasons that we were not the traditional 'perfect match.' Ann, nearly six years my senior, married me when I was just twenty one. Her mother was deeply concerned that she was marrying someone so young and void of any 'real job' prospects other than playing the trumpet. There were so many practical reasons why it was not a good idea, but God had a plan for our lives together. We truly believed that and we were in love.

His plan would include three children with red hair. I remember us constantly being questioned about how our three kids ended up with red hair. Frankly, we were more surprised than anyone else. When Joy was born, we chalked up the red hair to chance as we both had some cousins with red hair. When our son Jim was born (also with red hair), we were stunned but thankful for the 'matching set' God had blessed us with. When our third child, Faith, was also born with red hair we just could not believe it. My grandfather did have a full head of red hair and that generation skipping gene seemed to best explain our very Irish looking children.

After our first couple of years of marriage, I decided what I wanted to do with my life and pursued a career as a stockbroker. Times were not just good, but great. Money was pouring in and we enjoyed a wonderful lifestyle for many years. So much so that Ann was able to stop teaching and become a 'stay at home mom.' After starting my own business in the early 1990's our financial picture continued to just get brighter and brighter. In 2002, however, my situation dramatically took a turn for the worse when a relative embezzled nearly two million dollars from my businesses.

Our 'perfect life' was becoming a total disaster. I ended up in bankruptcy, we lost our home to foreclosure, and Ann ended up going back to work or we would have ended up homeless (no kidding). It was at the lowest of my lows that I truly realized how special my wife was. Ann told me that no matter how bad things got that she loved me and would stand by me. This assurance was without a doubt the only earthly thing I had to hold on to. If not for Ann I know I would have never made it through those very difficult years.

Twenty five years, a quarter century, two and a half decades... it has been a wild ride with lots of ups and downs. God gave me not just a wife but a best friend. When virtually everyone deserted me during my down years, Ann was there for me. They say you don't really know who your friends are until the chips are down (and I had completely run out of chips). In earthly terms, there were probably quite a lot of reasons why we were not a logical match but there is no question that our marriage was divine providence.

We were married at Grace Brethren Church on a Monday night in Long Beach, California, November 10, 1986. A wedding on a Monday night? Odd, but if we wanted a Saturday we would have had to wait over a year for an opening (its a California thing). God delivered into my life an amazing blessing and today, twenty five years later, I thank Him so much for Ann.

I love you Ann! Ready for another 25? –Jim"

COMING TO GRIPS WITH MY UNRAVELING FINANCIAL SITUATION

The first issue was that of our two cars. We reached the point of being two months behind on our car payments. What would we do without cars? I knew that it was inevitable that the cars would be repossessed. Rather than facing the humiliation of a tow truck coming to pick up the cars from our driveway, I contacted the finance companies and made arrangements to drop the cars back off at the dealerships where I bought them.

I will never forget taking my Cadillac back to the dealer in Daytona Beach to turn it in. There was a person I was to ask for by name, and when I pulled up I was able to quickly locate him. I handed him both sets of keys and he could see that this was an emotional moment for me. He asked me what happened and why I was returning the car. I gave him the 'Readers Digest' version of my story in about sixty seconds. With the utmost kindness, he said, "These things happen to the best people. Don't worry, you will be back to buy another Cadillac from us at some point in the future." This was a total stranger, but he offered me a moment of comfort that I will never forget.

I was able to find a used car in the local classifieds for my wife for $1,500. There were no frills, but it was a reliable car with air conditioning and we actually ended up keeping that little Buick Century for several years. My mom and dad had an extra car that they did not use very often, a small Ford pick up truck. I am not a pick up truck kind of a guy, but it provided transportation for me for more than a year until I could buy a car of my own.

The crisis of losing our cars was quickly behind us. I could not believe how worried I was about this and how easily it seemed that the problem was resolved. The takeaway from this is how we often times make problems out to be much larger than they really are. Sure, our credit was destroyed and we were not driving our dream cars, but life would go on.

It would take almost a year, but we would eventually lose our home to foreclosure. Losing the house was a big topic of discussion between my wife and I. What would we do? Where would we live? Would anyone even rent to us with our bad credit? There were lots of sleepless nights and worry tied up into the inevitable loss of our home. I was heartbroken when my daughter Faith, six years old at the time, came into my home office one morning and asked, "Daddy are we going to get to keep the house? Mommy and I have been praying." I told her that it was all in God's hands. I tried to hold myself together for a moment, and after she left I closed the door and cried like I never had before in my life. How could God be letting this happen to my family? Why would my brother do this to us and put our lives in such dire straits? There was not much time for crying or soul searching as the problems were coming at me like balls being thrown from a pitching machine.

With the foreclosure sale date fast approaching, there were busy days of packing and looking for a home to rent. It dawned on me that this was the first time in my life I was moving not by my own choice. I had relocated plenty of times. Each time involved perusing the real estate listings, meeting with Realtors, my wife and I taking property tours, etc. There was none of that this time as we were simply trying to find a roof to have over our heads. My wife asked me, "Do you think there is a chance we could end up homeless?" She then followed up with the belief that someone in her family would likely take us in until we found a home to rent. The problem with that was her closest relative was five hundred miles away. I just could not even believe that we were having a conversation discussing the possibility of becoming homeless, but it was happening.

We could not move in with my parents as my brother and his family had already done so. Not only had he wiped us out financially, but he had claimed first dibs on moving his own family in with my parents. This did cause a very serious strain between me and my parents, but I realized that they still loved my brother as their son, despite what he had done. My parents, as you can imagine, were devastated by what had happened. This was far greater than an issue of money; the embezzlement had torn our family completely apart.

We did find a wonderful home to rent, but I remember feeling so guilty about the foreclosure. After moving all of our stuff, my wife and I meticulously cleaned the house before it went back to the bank. Friends had suggested we remove our expensive lighting fixtures as we had added them to the property after we bought it. I decided that was just not right. I did not want to leave the bank with wires hanging from the ceiling and no lighting fixtures. The house was cleaned and I called the bank and asked them how they wanted me to turn over the key. They asked that I leave the front door unlocked and leave the key on the kitchen counter. I remember taking the last walk through the house by myself to make sure we had not forgotten anything and that nothing else needed to be cleaned or repaired prior to leaving. With the electric already turned off, it was so quiet I could hear myself breathing and the accelerating beating of my own heart. The silence was deafening.

My mind was instantly filled with all of the memories of the house. I looked out through the sliding glass doors at the pool and could vividly remember all of the parties we hosted on our deck, and the wonderful times of playing with the kids in the swimming pool. Each room had its own memories, especially the children's bedrooms. As I walked through each of their rooms I felt like such a failure as a father, believing that

I had let them down. I was just numb and simply said to myself, "I guess that is it, it is time to go." I placed the key on the kitchen counter and slowly walked out to my car to leave the house for the last time.

I remember arriving at the rental a few minutes later and the buzz and excitement that was going on. The kids could each have their own bedroom at the rental house and they were passionately arguing over who would get what room. As it turned out, the girls would also have their own bathroom and so would my son. I was really confused, never imagining that it would be like this. Losing the house wasn't really that bad after all, and my kids were so resilient. They had already moved on from losing our home to decorating their new rooms. My son had already mounted his mini basketball hoop and was taking twenty foot jump shots from across the kitchen.

My worst fears came true, but life was going on. Not only was life going on, but my children ended up being completely thrilled with the rental house. I had to stop myself and realize what was happening here. The Lord was there with us meeting our needs, providing not just another house but an even nicer house than what we had before. My kids were so excited, they would have never wanted to go back to the foreclosed house at this point. I was learning such a huge lesson in all of this.

The God of the universe, my provider, Jehovah Jireh, was gathering my family up in his arms and taking care of us.

One of the problems with being such a self-reliant person is that I never gave God much of a chance to step up for me and be my provider. I was *my own provider* and I believed that I would make sure that my family was always taken care of. There were so many blessings and lessons here it is impossible to share them all.

My wife was adamant that our kids would continue to attend their Christian school. The tuition was $1,000 monthly and I just saw no way that we could afford it on Ann's teacher salary and the little I was earning. Ann could not let this go; this was her last stand. "No matter what," she said "they are not going to be pulled out of their Christian school." Reality set in, and Ann and I had to accept that without my regular paycheck we could not afford to keep them in the school they had been attending. It was not especially good timing as it was already six weeks into the school year. The situation was clear, and we had no choice.

Jimmy and Faith were moved into a very nice public K-5 school not very far from the home we were renting. It was not their Christian school, but just like with the house, they were adjusting to the change just fine.

Things did not look so promising at the middle school our oldest would end up attending. It was a rough school - there is no other way to describe it. I remember driving my precious Joy to school for her first day. In the parking lot there were kids dressed like hoods, one with purple hair, kids kissing passionately, it really had the look of an inner city high school (and it was just a middle school). This was not at all like the single file lines of kids with matching school uniforms I would see at the Christian school. I was horrified. My daughter was going into what looked like a prison, I thought.

We had discussed home schooling with Joy, but she really wanted to attend school with other children and this was the public school we were zoned for. I realized that she could sense how upset I was, although I tried to hide my emotions. As I dropped her off, I will never forget her saying, "Dad, I will be OK here, don't worry." The tears began to well up in my eyes but I fought them off long enough for her not to see me crying. I remember getting about a block away and having to pull off to the side of the road to compose myself before I could continue the drive home. How could God let this happen? My beautiful, precious daughter was being thrown into the lion's den.

A few days went by and Joy was thriving at her new school. She became involved in a number of activities, including the music program. In truth, the school turned out not to be as bad as I had initially thought it was. Sure, there were some colorful characters there, but overall it was not really a bad school. I believe this was not just another lesson for Ann and I, but God was using all of this to prepare Joy.

Joy is an amazing person. In fact, I can't think of anyone else quite like her that I have ever known. At the time of writing this book, she is a full time college student, works in my Internet coaching business full time, and is a worship leader at a local church in St. Augustine. I realized years later that Joy faced adversity in her life just like I did when my dad became disabled after his construction accident. Like me, Joy is a survivor and very self reliant. She is an amazing problem solver and can make friends with just about anyone she meets. Her real passion, however, is music. Joy has recorded her own album and has toured in the United States and Europe with the Continental Singers (*www.joyparismusic.com*). More than anything, Joy has a heart for God. I could describe her no better to you than to simply make reference to her name.

Just like me, during her high school years, Joy had a number of jobs to be able to pay for all of the extras that Ann and I could not provide. At the time it seemed like God was really letting us down, but now I see how

He was using all of this to mold Joy into the person she is today.

I am often reminded of the lyrics of The Laura Story song, Blessings -

> *"'Cause what if your blessings come through raindrops. What if Your healing comes through tears. What if a thousand sleepless nights are what it takes to know You're near. What if trials of this life are Your mercies in disguise"*

Despite having resolved the car and house issues, my biggest problems were yet to come. About three years before my financial collapse, we began planning for a major expansion of our business. This involved raising a first round of venture capital, with the plans of taking the companies public. When the companies discontinued operations due to the financial collapse, outside investors owned approximately ten percent of the stock in my money management firm and publishing company.

I remember the day I sat down and wrote a letter to our investors explaining the embezzlement. I asked each person to forgive me and I sincerely apologized for what had happened. I had no secretary at this point - I typed the letter myself, printed it out, stuffed about eighty envelopes, signed each letter, added a stamp, and drove them down to the post office. I was so worried about how these letters would be received.

About a week later, the letters in response starting arriving. I had our mail moved to a UPS store in Daytona Beach since I no longer had an official office address. I sat quietly in the parking lot in my car and my hands trembled as I began to open the letters. One by one they shared words of encouragement, told me they were praying for me, that they forgave me, I simply could not believe it! I was expecting the absolute worst and again I was wrong.

The reality was, however, that not everyone was so gracious. There were a handful of investors that would not accept what had happened. After making complaints to state regulators, I was being investigated for 'securities fraud.' The suspicion was that my claim about my brother embezzling the money was just a ruse and that I had really taken the money myself.

I know this sounds completely ridiculous. Why in the world would I destroy my own companies, end up losing my home, my income, everything I had worked for? It made no sense, but I had to work through three years of an investigation nonetheless. I remember being so upset that I would have episodes of throwing up blood that would last several hours at a time. The truth is that I just wanted to die. I had no relief, even when I would sleep I would have nightmares about what was happening. I could handle losing all of my money, the house, the cars, but not this. I was afraid to even talk to my securities lawyer, as he would always begin by reminding me how much money I owed him and ask me when he was going to get paid. My life was literally a living hell and I believed I had come up with a final solution; I would kill myself.

PLANNING MY OWN SUICIDE

I am ashamed to admit it, but on three separate occasions I planned my own suicide in detail. I even went so far as to review my life insurance polices to make sure that they would pay off after my suicide. Thank God I never went through with it, but I came very close. I was a complete and utter emotional wreck and death seemed like a much better option than the onslaught of problems I had to wake up to every morning. I was dead broke, had to work sixty hours a week on simply getting through my bankruptcy and the investigation. As much as I needed money, I had little time to work outside of what had become my full time job: dealing with my financial mess.

I was not one to go to counselors or therapists, but Ann insisted. She was a teacher and had great medical benefits, and I could see a psychiatrist for $20 per visit. I remember sharing my story during my first one hour appointment. The doctor, cupping his chin in his hand repeatedly, said, "Your own brother...your own brother." I could surmise that a story like mine was not like any he had heard before. I was evaluated for Post Traumatic Stress Disorder. I had heard of this condition before, but thought it was only related to people that had gone to war. In the end, my diagnosis was off the charts for PTSD. The nightmares, the flashbacks, the anxiety attacks, I was a textbook case of PTSD. I was able to get help from Dr. Raphael Parlade (to whom this book is dedicated – more on this in chapter six).

I wanted to move on with my life and take any job I could get. I went down to the DMV and took the test to become a taxi driver, went on a couple of interviews, but never took a taxi job. I ended up working for a year in my sister's mortgage brokerage office as a clerk for $400 per week. I was earning less than I paid my secretarial staff, but I was glad to have a job. Later I was able to obtain a mortgage license of my own and worked for her as a mortgage broker for a short time before doing so independently from a small office in Daytona Beach. There was no mountain of money here. I would typically earn $2,000 to $3,000 monthly after expenses. It was nothing like the income I had before, but with

Ann's income as a school teacher, we were doing just fine.

Perhaps the biggest part of my story is the point in 2005 when I eventually had to file for bankruptcy. Here is a blog post I wrote about that experience -

"As a Christian finance writer, there are two topics that I approach with great fear; divorce and bankruptcy. I remember in my early days as a Christian writer receiving a letter from a pastor scolding me for including a chapter on divorce and finances in one of my books. The letter not only shared his disappointment in me for allegedly making divorce easier for people, he added that he would never buy any of my books and that I was banned from being a speaker at his church. Despite my best efforts, and several paragraphs of disclaimers making clear that I was not advocating divorce, some readers would never forgive me for broaching the topic. I have run into many of the same hurdles when addressing the issue of bankruptcy. If I offer understanding and compassion to a caller in bankruptcy during a live radio show, I need not wait more than about five minutes to start seeing an influx of e mails rebuking me and even questioning my salvation. I have struggled for years wondering why Christians are so judgmental about bankruptcy.

In 2005 I was given the opportunity, first-hand, to have an in-depth education on bankruptcy; *I* was going bankrupt. I became completely convinced that this would be the death of my Christian financial writing and speaking career. This time, I was not offering grace and understanding to someone else going through bankruptcy; it was me. My accountant informed me in the Spring of 2002 that my brother Carmen Paris (who was our internal accountant) had been embezzling from me for several years. The amount lost was ultimately estimated to be approximately 2 million dollars, although I stopped counting after going through five years of bank records.

I remember the day I was required to go to federal bankruptcy court in Jacksonville, Florida. It is a large white building with plenty of granite and marble in the entrance way. Everything about this place screamed out intimidation. About two hundred of us soon-to-be-bankrupt individuals were herded into a dimly lit room. We were to wait as our name was called and then go to the front of the room and sit at a long table. At the other end of the table was the bankruptcy trustee. He explained that it was his job to represent the creditors in our bankruptcy. As each person was seated they were asked about five to ten questions. In my case, the process took almost twenty minutes, which seemed like an eternity. 'Now, Mr. Paris, why are you filing for bankruptcy?' I was asked. The trustee seemed extremely interested, especially when it came out that I was a financial writer. 'A financial writer; so what was the title of your most recent book?' I answered, *Money Management For Those Who Don't Have Any* which caused us all to start laughing, to which I added, 'How ironic, huh?'

Talk about humiliating; this was about as bad as it could get. After I was excused, I sat back down in the back of the room to gather together all of my personal papers and I saw an elderly man go up to take his place at the table. He was steadied on either side by two younger individuals that appeared to be his adult children. The man could hardly speak he was crying so uncontrollably. For a moment, my problems seemed trivial compared to the heartbreak I was witnessing. The man explained through his tears how he could not pay his medical bills, and in order to save his mobile home, he was filing for bankruptcy. There is a generation of our population that still views bankruptcy as perhaps the largest personal failing one can have in life. This man was losing far more than money, it looked like life itself was being wrenched from his body. Tears began to well up in my own eyes as I left the courthouse. I had to wonder how anyone could not have compassion on such a soul as this?

As I walked to the street I recognized a young man who had been called up to the table about a half hour before me. I remember him sharing his story of a job loss, medical bills, and his home being in foreclosure. He was sitting on a bench in the park with his head in his hands, apparently crying for quite some time. As I looked over his shoulder I saw him holding a small booklet that said, 'Jesus Cares.' Perhaps a good samaritan handed this to him while passing by and witnessing his grief. How can we do anything but love and care for these people? How can we sit in judgment of them in our piousness? How can any of us be so confident that we may not end up in similar circumstances?

As I wrestle with this topic, I am continually drawn back to the spiritual parallel that God has placed in my heart. We, being sinners unable to pay our debt, go to God through Jesus Christ to ask for forgiveness. I truly believe that at the foundation of our Christian faith is what I call spiritual bankruptcy. If we can accept the premise that God can forgive us for our spiritual debt, why can we not offer grace to those who face financial bankruptcy? Even the Lord's Prayer (Matthew 6:9-13) makes reference to the forgiveness of debts. Of course many will say this is not a financial debt and respond with Psalm 37:21 The wicked borrow and do not pay back. I am not a theologian, but I cannot believe that somehow financial shortcomings, even those that were the result of outright sin or bad decisions, cannot be forgiven. Not forgiving those who have had financial failings seems like a clearly unbiblical stance, but one that still seems to make the rounds today. In my view, the wicked referenced in Psalm 37 would be today's version of those committing financial fraud. Borrowing with no intention of repaying, or not repaying a debt when you have the ability to do so, seems like the principle at issue here.

I confess, there was a time in my early thirties that I looked around at my estate home, new cars, closet filled with designer suits, my six figure income, my red Corvette, and thought I was financially invincible. I was prideful and believed that things would just keep getting better. Despite losing all of my material wealth, I have to concede that I like the Jim Paris of today much more than the old one.

I don't know if it was good for me to have had a bankruptcy, but I know that, as Christians, we are promised that all things can be used for good for those that love God and those that are called according to His purpose (Romans 8:28). I believe that God has used my bankruptcy to change me for the better. Rather than use my bankruptcy as a reason to stop my Christian financial teaching, I have chosen to embrace it. This is now another opportunity for me to relate with those facing life's most difficult financial challenges and to continue to keep my heart soft when pride threatens to return."

PURSUING MY BROTHER LEGALLY FOR THE EMBEZZLEMENT

In order to ultimately clear my own name and put an end to the securities fraud investigation, I had to prove once and for all that my brother had embezzled the money, and this would turn out to be a Herculean task. The logical starting point I thought would be our accounting firm. Since they discovered the embezzlement initially, I thought they could help me to piece this all together. I was shocked when they said that they did not want to be involved and that I was on my own. They explained that they did not want the liability involved with accusing someone of embezzlement. I pointed out to them that they had already made the accusation, I just needed their help putting all of the documents together. It would make no difference, they washed their hands of the situation. I quickly learned that the 'dead broke' Jim Paris had few friends left.

So how hard could it be to gather together all of the bank records and start accounting for what had happened? After all, I was a financial guy and this did not seem like all that difficult of a project. Unfortunately, I discovered our banking and financial records were missing and I was shocked to see empty shelves where the records would normally be kept. In an attempt to cover his tracks, my brother had taken our bank records going back ten years. Several employees had later informed me that they witnessed him taking a large number of file boxes to his car on his last day at our Apopka, FL office. Everyone assumed that they were just part of the process of him cleaning out his own personal office.

Well, I would just have to go to the banks directly and get copies of the account records. This turned out, however, to be a very expensive nightmare. First, we had several banking relationships in both Florida and Texas. Next, I found out that obtaining historical records would cost a significant amount of money, and it would take time. It took several months and several thousand dollars to pay the banks to reproduce the account records. Fortunately, I still had money trickling in from residual profits on the businesses, and without any overhead I was able to scrape the money together to pay for the bank records.

What I discovered when going through the bank records was beyond shocking. I remember becoming physically sick when reviewing each set of bank documents that would arrive. Both the amounts and the frequency of withdrawals that my brother was taking from the businesses were hard to believe, and even harder to imagine how our accounting firm did not catch on to this sooner. My attorney was adamant that the only way to clear my own name was to prove that my brother, and not I, had taken the money out of the businesses. These bank records would prove to be the key to that.

My brother, using the money he had stolen, 'lawyered up' and would not talk to me or answer any questions about the missing bank records. On top of that, he was living rent free at my parent's home. I was at such a huge disadvantage, but I knew that God was on my side. I went to various law enforcement agencies, spending countless hours providing them with documentation on the embezzlement. The local police determined that it was 'too big' of a case for them and set up an appointment for me to go to the FBI. I provided all of the details and documentation to the FBI and after two interviews with them at their Maitland, FL office, they informed me that my case was 'too small' for them to get involved with. Next, I was referred to the Florida Department of Law Enforcement. Yep, you guessed it... the case was 'too big' for them to get involved.

It was hard to conceive how someone could embezzle this amount of money and not be prosecuted. I have, over the years, had my antennae up for embezzlement stories in the news. It does seem like a crime that is often just sporadically prosecuted. My attorney explained that I would have had more of a chance getting a prosecution if my brother had stolen a television set from my house. This was a very discouraging lesson to learn about our 'justice' system.

HOW I ACCIDENTALLY UNCOVERED A SERIOUS CONFLICT OF INTEREST

My sister's husband told me that my brother came over to their house and that he had been drinking heavily. He was bragging about how he had 'rigged' the case against me with the State of Florida and how he had worked it out that he would avoid any consequences himself. His demeanor, as it was described to me, was that he was laughing uncontrollably as he shared his scheme. He explained that the attorney he hired was a former employee of the very office of the State of Florida office of Financial Regulation that was investigating me. My brother also claimed that his attorney was a close personal friend of the individual heading the investigation.

What was astonishing to discover was that I was able to confirm much of his story to be true. His attorney had worked for that agency and that exact office for several years prior to going into private practice. The individual handling my investigation was also employed in that same office during those years. Wow, my head was really spinning trying to comprehend what was happening here. Was I being set up? How could this be happening and what could I do about it?

Having this information would turn out to be a real breakthrough in my legal case. Within a day of learning all of this, I had also finished the several month process of assembling the bank records that would prove my brother's embezzlement. I immediately called my attorney with an update. He insisted that I come to his office for a meeting the very next day. I had never heard him so angry. He went into a wild tirade filled with four letter words. He said, "I will have this guy disbarred and maybe even put in jail. So this is why they have refused to listen to what I have been telling them." My attorney had explained to me that for months he was unable to get the state investigators to consider the facts about my brother. Now it was all starting to add up.

I don't know nor can I prove that there was any corruption in the way that my case was handled. I do know that when confronted with the information I had learned from my brother-in-law, the office investigating me dramatically changed their tune. My attorney made just one phone call and I was told to report to the office of Financial Regulation the next day with my twenty three pound box of bank documents proving my brother's embezzlement. Within a matter of days, the investigation against me was completely dropped. I know that the Lord was truly protecting me in all of this. My attorney said that he believed that my brother had agreed to testify against me and that I may have been indicted. If not for his slip of the tongue, and my recreating the banking documents, I could have ended up being convicted of securities fraud and gone to prison for five to ten years. Even more shocking, the office of Financial Regulation never pursued my brother even after they learned that he was the real bad guy. My attorney said they were likely too embarrassed about what would have come out if they continued on with the case.

As of this writing, Carmen Paris, inexplicably, has never been, nor likely will ever be, criminally charged by the State of Florida office of Financial Regulation or any other regulatory or law enforcement agency for embezzling nearly two million dollars from me and several dozen investors.

To their credit, the National Association of Securities Dealers (now known as the Financial Industry Regulatory Authority, or FINRA) did their own parallel investigation of my brother's shady accounting practices surrounding the embezzlement. As a result, he received a lifetime ban from the securities industry. Known as the 'death penalty,' this is the most severe civil penalty that a securities regulator can issue. It would not mean any jail time, but would likely keep him out of any regulated profession in the future.

ONE FINAL ISSUE STILL NEEDING TO BE RESOLVED

Although my brother could never work again in the securities industry, it was important to me that I obtain some type of official declaration that he had embezzled the money. The NASD sanction was for accounting irregularities and not directly for the embezzlement. What was especially upsetting was that a number of my own extended family members would say things like, "Well, that is your story and your brother has his story." This was not right what he had done. Not only to me and my family, but also the investors that lost money.

THE FINAL SHOWDOWN WITH MY BROTHER

I could not believe that no law enforcement agency was going to prosecute my brother, but I had to accept that I had done all that I could and I had no control over their decision. My only option to ultimately clear my name, and get some measure of justice, was to file a civil lawsuit. No, my brother would not go to jail, but I could get a court to make it official that he did embezzle the money. For years he continued to deny everything. No apologies, no remorse, and I was just not going to let things end this way. It was not about revenge, but justice.

I was short on money, but had just received a royalty check for about $4,000 owed to me for past sales of my books. I called up my longtime friend, attorney David Ferguson in Ormond Beach, FL. David was already aware of my financial collapse and was only too happy to help. I told him that I had $4,000 and that was all I could pay him to represent me in the lawsuit against my brother. In June of 2005, with David's help, I filed suit on behalf of myself and my corporations. I was unsure what would happen next.

How would my brother respond? This was the first time that I would have had the chance to legally confront him about the embezzlement, and more than four years had passed. I thought maybe he would just not answer the lawsuit and I would win by default. I watched as the twenty day time limit for a response approached. With just two days left to file a response, he did. This may be the most shocking part of my story yet.

He denied all of my allegations of the embezzlement and then filed a counter claim against me for $100,000. Yes, he was suing me! My attorney explained that this is a very common tactic in a lawsuit. It may be common, but I simply could not believe it. What more could my brother do to me at this point? How long would this all take? Could there be some scenario where I could end up owing him money at the end of this?

I met with David Ferguson to discuss the case a few weeks later. We decided that the first thing that we should do is to force my brother to answer questions under oath, so a deposition was scheduled. David and I both believed that he would not show up for the deposition as we were prepared to confront him with the bank documents and require him to explain the unauthorized withdrawals. In the end, that is what happened. My brother's attorney called the day before the deposition to cancel and informed us that they were going to concede the case. The lawsuit was over and the judge awarded me $4.7 million dollars!

I never received any money from the judgment, as it became an asset of my bankruptcy. It was never about the money anyway. I had accomplished the one thing that I so desperately wanted; I cleared my name. There was no longer any question about what happened. I was the victim of an embezzlement scheme and my brother was the perpetrator.

FINDING PEACE THROUGH FORGIVENESS

I would be lying if I told you that I was not harboring anger in my heart and even hate toward my brother. Not just because of what he had done to me, but especially because of the misery his actions caused my wife and children. The years passed and no apology was received. I have never been one to place a lot of significance on biblical numbers, although I know that they are legitimately part of Bible history. I had been hearing for a few weeks about the 8/08/08 date and what Christians were saying about it. The number eight is widely accepted by Bible commentators as God's number for *new beginnings*.

I remember feeling led by the Lord to forgive my brother. For years I had been harboring resentment and anger and I knew that this was something the Lord wanted me to do. How could I forgive him, when he had still not apologized or even admitted what he had done? I could not control what he would do, but

I could decide to forgive him and that was within my power. I wrote a very simple letter to my brother letting him know that I completely forgave him.

Here is the text of that letter -

Friday, August 08, 2008

Carmen,
Today is my last step in a very long journey. Even though you continue to deny what you have done and you have never apologized, my Lord has told me to forgive you. You are forgiven, you owe me nothing.

Sincerely,
Jim
Ephesians 4:32

After I finished writing the letter, I really had second thoughts and considered throwing it away. I let it sit on my desk for several days and reviewed it over and over again. I needed to do this, it was what God wanted me to do. There was one last thing that I felt was necessary before mailing the letter. It was August 8, 2008, a Friday. I had called my wife at work and told her that as soon as she got home from school I needed her to go somewhere with me. She repeatedly queried me about where we were going. I simply explained that I would give her the details when she got home that afternoon.

When Ann arrived home we drove to our local post office. I had the letter I had written to my brother in my glove compartment. I pulled into a parking space and took the letter out and handed it to her. With tears streaming down my face, I explained to her that I had to do this. I had to send this letter of forgiveness but couldn't do it without her blessing. Ann hugged me and we both cried for several minutes and she knew that it took a lot for me to want to do this. We had both been in such a survival state for so many years, it was a beautiful thought that this just might be our *new beginning*. With Ann by my side, I drove up to the mailbox and dropped the letter in before the final pick up.

I did not expect any response from my brother and none was received, although I did confirm through my mom that he had, in fact, received the letter. The letter was dated August 8, 2008, and postmarked with that date, as well, and I was accepting this as the first day of the rest of our lives.

THE WINDOWS OF HEAVEN OPENED UP

That letter was truly the beginning of so many blessings for us. My business partner, Bob Yetman, and I had just launched our online school on Internet marketing. The business began to grow more quickly than we had ever expected. A real boost to our growth were major media appearances on Daystar TV, Point of View Radio, and The Christian Television Network. The traffic and interest in our main website, ChristianMoney.com, was off the charts. Moody Radio Chicago invited me to be a regular guest every Wednesday on their morning drive radio program. I was doing seminars again to rooms filled with people! God was restoring me and giving me another chance to pursue my life's passion of helping Christians with their finances. This was truly a miracle! A miracle that I believe was released when I followed the Lord's leading to forgive my brother.

My wife would receive an inheritance shortly after this which provided the money for our family to own our own home again, and without a mortgage!

LOSING ONE BROTHER BUT GAINING ANOTHER

A major part of my story would be missing if I did not shed light on the very special friendship I have with my business partner Bob Yetman. Many of you know him as the co-host of the various podcasts we produce each month. I hired Bob as an entry level financial adviser in the late 1980's when I was a vice president at a nationwide financial planning firm in Orlando. Later, Bob would come to work for me when I formed my own businesses in the early 1990's. I remember when I closed down my businesses not having the money to pay much of his final payroll. I offered to give him our phone system in lieu of his final paycheck and he graciously agreed.

Bob and I continued to work together on a wide variety of projects over the years. He is a very talented writer and edits virtually everything I write (including this book). We are really more like family than business partners. In fact, I consider him the brother that I gained in all of this. Believe me, no one would mistake us as being biological brothers, which is why I explain that we are 'financial brothers.' I have often made reference to the movie 'Twins' in which Arnold Schwarzenegger and Danny Devito are paired as twin brothers in this hilarious comedy. If you met the two of us in person, you would quickly surmise that I play the role of Devito in our similarly unlikely pairing as brothers.

LOSING MY FATHER

In September of 2011 my father went to be with the Lord. He had been in failing health on and off again for several years. The medications that he relied on to manage the pain from his back injury had caused irreversible damage to many of his vital organs. It was very awkward, but I did see my brother at the funeral service. He waited until the very end of the service, and the final moment before the casket was closed. He whispered over my father's body, saying, "Jimmy, I am sorry for everything I did." My dad had begged him to apologize to me for years and I know he wanted to do this for my dad. I know my dad was smiling in heaven. They were merely words, words that have never been followed by any actions evidencing true redemption. Nonetheless, I was glad the words were spoken as a tribute to my father's last wish on earth.

CONCLUSION

We never know where life will take us and my life has been filled with lots of twists and turns and I know that there will be more of them to come. There is no promise in the Bible that we, as Christians, will not face adversity. We can have confidence in knowing that the Lord will be with us in life's valleys and that he is standing by to provide us with comfort and wisdom in dealing with our daily challenges.

CHAPTER FIVE

Praying For Your Financial Miracle

I have already braced myself for the expected criticism I will undoubtedly receive for using the world 'miracle' throughout this book, including in the title. There are those that would disagree with my perspective that someone finding a job that has been out of work for months, or accumulating the money to get caught up on their mortgage, or pay an overdue medical bill, are actually the beneficiaries of true miracles. After all, aren't miracles supposed to be big events, like raising the dead? I guess these may only be considered miracles by those facing such dire circumstances.

"It's a recession when your neighbor loses his job;
it's a depression when you lose your own."
–HARRY S. TRUMAN.

What I am about to delve into in this chapter is something that will absolutely change your life. Imagine stepping out in faith, and I mean really stepping out and trusting God for answers to your current financial challenges. Let me share with you a blog post I wrote a few years ago which outlines an approach to financial prayer that I believe the Lord revealed to me.

> *"If any of you lacks wisdom, he should ask
> God who gives generously to all ..."*
> –JAMES 1:5 (NIV)

"What is intelligence? I recently completed an Intelligence Quotient test and was required to answer questions comparing series of shapes, calculation of distances, and even such questions as, "Hand is to glove as sock is to…" (if you guessed foot, you would have gotten that one right). After completing the exam, I was given my "I.Q. score" and information regarding my ranking against the overall population. This whole experience really made me wonder what intelligence is. There are as many definitions of "smart" as there are people attempting to define it. Some are considered "street smart," others "book smart," and yet others are said to have "good common sense."

In real life terms, our ability to solve everyday problems is probably the most practical application of our intellectual abilities. Wisdom is defined by Webster as "good sense." The best definition I have heard is, "wisdom is the application of knowledge." In other words, wisdom is the transformation of the knowing into the doing.

> *"The only true wisdom is knowing you know nothing."*
> –SOCRATES

The Bible frequently references wisdom, which is an attribute far deeper than one's I.Q. or ability to solve math problems. The King James Version of the Bible includes 234 references to wisdom. What must we do then to become wise? Is it a matter of education, life experience, our parents? While I am sure that we each have obtained some measure of earthly wisdom from these experiences, real wisdom comes only from God. The exciting thing about obtaining wisdom, is that it's there for the asking! God promises to give us wisdom if we would only ask him for it.

My greatest prayer for those that I counsel is for God to grant them wisdom. Wisdom is more than just an answer for today's problems, it is our ongoing ability to respond to everyday challenges. While libraries and bookstores are filled with thousands of financial books, reading them all will only provide knowledge. Knowledge, while important and necessary, is like a rocket without fuel. Wisdom is the ability to pull together this raw information and synthesize it into a practical application for your life today.

A challenge in wisdom: find a quiet place and provide yourself with a minimum of two hours. During these two hours, bring only a pen and a notepad. Ask your family not to disturb you during this exercise. Begin by asking God for wisdom. Next, make a list of your financial problems. Go ahead, keep listing them even if it takes several pages to do so. Lastly, look over your list of "problems" and prioritize them. You might do this by making a new list and ranking them from most important to least important. An alternative would be to give each problem a rating such as "L" for low, "M" for medium, and "H" for high. You should have at least sixty to ninety minutes left to "brainstorm." Start by placing each one of your high priority problems at the top of a separate sheet of paper. Now, sit quietly and truly seek answers from God.

As solutions come to mind, write them down on the sheet of paper corresponding to that problem. Don't question, don't think of all of the reasons that a given idea won't work, just write them down. After you have completed this exercise, you will have dozens if not hundreds of solutions to your most urgent problems. Repeat this exercise often, taking time to deal with your medium and low level issues before they move up in the ranking. This approach also works well for *any* problem, financial or otherwise.

What is wonderful about this method is that we are literally giving God our problems, asking for His wisdom, and then offering a blank pad of paper for His solutions. Why don't we just stop our busy lives and ask God for His wisdom and guidance? God is waiting right now for you to ask."

THE FINANCIAL MIRACLE PRAYER

Let us unpack the above prayer and get down to brass tacks as to how you can begin using it right away. First, let's be honest about the reality that in many cases we have, through our own bad decisions and poor choices, created our own financial problems. Many times the roots of our financial failures can be found in making the mistake of presuming the future.

> *Now listen, you who say, "Today or tomorrow we will go to this or that city, spend a year there, carry on business and make money." Why, you do not even know what will happen tomorrow. What is your life? You are a mist that appears for a little while and then vanishes. Instead, you ought to say, "If it is the Lord's will, we will live and do this or that." As it is, you boast in your arrogant schemes. All such boasting is evil. If anyone, then, knows the good they ought to do and doesn't do it, it is sin for them.*
>
> –JAMES 4:13-17 (NIV)

While it may seem easier to paint yourself as a victim, I think it is a healthy starting point to search your heart and be very honest about what missteps you have made that have contributed to your current predicament. I think this accomplishes two things. First, it is a great exercise that will be a future reminder for you not to repeat these same mistakes. Secondly, it is an excellent opportunity to start your prayer by asking the Lord to forgive you for whatever part you played in your financial mess. I believe this is a perfect way to begin your own prayer seeking a financial miracle. In my own case, I can certainly blame my brother, but I also have to take a large amount of the blame myself. I was not monitoring closely enough what was happening with the finances of my businesses. This blame falls squarely on my own shoulders. If I had been paying closer attention, I would have uncovered the embezzlement years earlier and may have had a chance to save my businesses.

The next part of the prayer should be focused on all of the things you are grateful for and all of the blessings you already have. For me, my problems look so much smaller when I consider all of my blessings. I have my health, a wonderful family, my basic needs are met, etc. Gratitude is something that most of us are deeply lacking today. If you think your problems are big, you don't have to go very far to find someone else struggling with multiples of what you have on your plate. I have caught myself feeling depressed about a business deal not coming together, and then hearing that a close friend has cancer. At that moment, I am so ashamed of how big of a fuss I made of my minor issue and can only think of my friend and what he is facing. If you really think about it, even the poorest in our society are still rich compared to how people live in most other parts of the world.

WHAT CAN YOU PRAY FOR?

I was just returning from lunch and was behind a car with a bumper sticker that said, "Pray For Surf." I live in a beachside community and good surf is a big deal for many of my neighbors. As far as I am concerned, you can approach God in prayer for anything that you need and even for things that you simply want. I have one big caveat in writing this: first and foremost, you should be seeking God's will for your life. Remember that the Lord's top priority is a relationship with us and to mold us into His character. At this point, we begin to really run across some major differences as to how people of different Christian denominations pray and what they pray for. If you flip through the TV channels (especially late at night), you will hear things like, "God wants you to be rich," "God wants you to have that new car, new house, or a million dollars in the bank." That is a very popular message and is usually followed by an appeal for the viewer to make a financial gift to that ministry personality's organization.

On the other end of the spectrum, we hear that money is evil and that the more of it we have, the more likely we are to drift away from God. These views represent the two extremes - prosperity and poverty theology, and both have missed the point. My view is that once we give our lives over to the Lord, everything we have belongs to Him. We are then managers or stewards of these *temporary* belongings. The stewardship concept is made clear throughout the New Testament and most especially in Matthew 25:14-30. Once you accept your role as simply a manager of God's property, it gives you a new perspective and will greatly influence how you approach the Lord in prayer.

OK, back to the prayer. We come to the Lord first with humility, accepting responsibility for our own failings (and asking for forgiveness) and we thank him for all the He has already done for us. Next, we pray for His will to be done in our lives and in our current circumstances. We ask the Lord for wisdom in resolving our current financial predicament. Recognize the Lord as your provider and ask for His help in meeting your financial needs.

What happens next? Well, this is why I suggest in my blog post that you set aside an hour or two to be able to sit and listen quietly to the Lord for His direction. This is not easy for most of us to do, especially if you are a 'type A' personality like me that can hardly sit in one place for more than ten minutes. Leave your cell phone, computer, everything behind when you go to meet with the Lord in this way. Psalm 46:10 says "Be still and know that I am God...." In today's world of iPads, smart phones, and mobile computing, this is becoming more and more of a challenge. Can you give the Lord just one hour of your time?

THE MYTH OF MULTI-TASKING

What happens in your brain when you are multi-tasking is that you are actually switching back and forth between activities very quickly, so quickly that you don't even notice it. I am talking about 100% concentration here and giving God your highest and best level of attention. Multi-tasking will be counterproductive during the time you have set aside for your encounter with God. I am reminded of Matthew 26:40 where the disciples are chided for falling asleep when they were simply asked to stand watch for one hour while Jesus was praying.

THE LORD WILL SPEAK TO YOU!

We don't hear God because we are usually not listening. Your yellow pad will become so full with ideas and solutions, you simply won't believe it. Again, it is important that you don't question these ideas as they come to you. Begin writing each of them down as they come to mind. There will be time later for review, reflection, and additional prayer that will lead to your final direction.

People spend such little time thinking today. When something goes wrong, most of us call technical support, or a friend for advice, or perhaps do a Google search. I was at the bookstore the other day and was surprised at how many books there are on the topic of meditation. The idea of just sitting still, being quiet and reflective, is being sold as a 'success strategy' by many of the top name motivational gurus. What I am discussing here is not just sitting and 'emptying' your mind (as the far east religions would suggest); I am talking about opening up your mind to the Lord and listening to what He has to say to you.

BEING OPEN TO SOLUTIONS YOU MAY HAVE NEVER CONSIDERED BEFORE

It was the mid 1990's and I was in Pittsburgh to appear on a national Christian TV Network. The cab driver that took me to my hotel told me how bad things were in Pittsburgh, how hard it was to find a job, and how many people were struggling. I knew that Pittsburgh was a depressed city, and along the highway I saw a large number of abandoned factory sites. Steel factories, formerly the heart of the city, had been mostly closed down. I heard these same downtrodden stories from a couple of the workers at the hotel. Later that night I walked across the parking lot to a local steakhouse for dinner. I asked the server if things were so bad in Pittsburgh, why people didn't consider relocating. He looked at me like I had a plant growing out of my head and then just smiled and laughed. That was it; I never got an answer.

The next day I shared my experience with the driver from the TV network that came to pick me up. I told him about all of the people I had already met who had described Pittsburgh as an economic wasteland. I also told him about the reaction I got from my waiter the night before when I asked why people don't move to other cities where there may be better opportunities. My driver looked at me, smiled, and laughed. He said, "You just don't understand Pittsburgh people. People don't move from Pittsburgh," he explained. "If you are born here, you stay here." He really thought it was funny that I was even thinking about people moving to find jobs.

The point here is not to pick on Pittsburgh or its residents, but to really question why we are not willing to put everything on the table when we go to God for help. Although we don't really think of our prayers this way, many times we are saying, "Please help me Lord - but on my own terms." The idea of relocating for a job is something that a very large percentage of Americans do not even consider. At the time of writing this book, there are several cities with 100% employment! These may be cities you have never heard of, like Steubenville, OH and Williston, ND, which are both desperately seeking workers for high paying jobs in the oil and gas industries.

What's your point, Jim? I don't have any training or experience to work in the oil industry. Well, towns like this (and there are many) need teachers, police officers, home builders, cooks, daycare providers...the list is endless. Let's revisit the idea, though, that you are not a 'trained oil worker.' Who says you need to be trained? I would guess that, like in many trades, you could get some amount of on the job training. If not, you might get the training you need in a short window of time.

Consider the story of a friend of mine. While in his late thirties he decided to go back to college to get into the medical industry. After just eighteen months of college he became a respiratory therapist. He now owns his own respiratory therapy business that provides a wide range of services and delivers oxygen all over the city. He laughed when he told me that he walks around the hospital with a white jacket and stethoscope and earns as much as the doctors do after less than two years of college! There are so many opportunities like this that can be pursued within a small window of time in college or a vocational school. Adapting to the new economy may be part of your financial miracle.

About a year ago, just for fun, I took a computer repair class through our local adult education program. It was two hours, one night per week, for six weeks. After completing the course, I could take a desktop computer completely apart, add new drives, add memory...it was amazing. Through the class I learned enough to handle all of my own computer repairs. I also learned that to become officially certified through Microsoft to do basic computer repairs could be done in less than six months.

There are countless money making 'possibilities' like this. For example, what about relocating to a foreign country? Sounds a little crazy, but I have considered it myself. Right now, while millions of Americans are receiving unemployment, countries around the globe are in desperate need of English teachers. No English degree required, just take a forty hour class and you are certified to teach. Imagine the adventure of living in Europe, the Far East, or even South America for a year or more! Check out the website *www.makemoneyteaching.us* for a program I recommend.

I briefly touched on this in the introduction, but a fascinating and fast growing business is that of cleaning foreclosed homes. I recently did a podcast on this and was shocked to learn that people are earning $500 to $1,000 per day cleaning these abandoned homes for the banks. A training program I recommend on this is available at *www.foreclosurecleaning.us*.

For some people, in the interim, you may need to pick up a mundane income opportunity such as delivering pizzas, mowing lawns, or waiting tables. I remember my pastor in Chicago asking me where I was working. I was a teenager and had a menial job flipping hamburgers at the time. As I told him what I was doing, he could tell by my demeanor that I was not all that proud. He grabbed me by the shoulders and looked me in the eye and said, Don't ever be ashamed of an honest day of work. I am very proud of you." Wow, he was right, and that gave me a fresh perspective on the virtue of working.

The point of all of this is not to convince you that the answer in *your* life is moving, but to *get* moving. Start moving in the direction that God is leading you, wherever that may be. A new career, a new locale, downsizing to a smaller home, the list is endless. Put everything on the table, give Him your problems and also your willingness to go in whatever direction He leads.

HOW LONG BEFORE MY PRAYER IS ANSWERED?

God's time is not ours. In fact, He is on a completely different timeline than we are. In God's time, one day is the same as a thousand years and a thousand years is the same as a day (2 Peter 3:8). In some cases, you will see immediate results. During the several years of my financial crisis I saw God move with the speed of lightning, and in some cases it seemed like He was moving in slow motion. I hate to bring another cliché saying into the text of the book, but the reality is that some miracles do take time. It is no less of a miracle if it takes a few months or even years to come to fruition than if it happens instantaneously.

Here is a blog post, I wrote a few years back on this topic -

Perseverance, Survival While In The Midst of Trouble

"Blessed is the one who perseveres under trial because, having stood the test, that person will receive the crown of life that the Lord has promised to those who love him."
–James 1:12 (NIV)

"We live in a society of immediate gratification. We have little patience for slow fast food, long lines at the grocery store or even the three minutes it takes to cook a bag of popcorn in the microwave oven. Just as we expect our every day conveniences to be provided to us instantaneously, we want immediate answers to our financial problems. Webster's definition for perseverance is 'to persist in a state, enterprise, or undertaking in spite of counter influences, opposition, or discouragement.' In other words, don't give up when things get tough."

"Most people give up just when they're about to achieve success. They quit on the one yard line. They give up at the last minute of the game one foot from a winning touchdown."
–Ross Perot

The most difficult part of any problem is the middle. The first stage tends to leave most of us in shock and not able to really feel the pain. Of course, the conclusion of a problem is fantastic and the feeling of relief is incomparable. The middle point of our financial challenge is when perseverance becomes reality. It is at this point that we are deep in the dark tunnel, but not far enough along yet to see any light at the other end.

Some things just take time, and some financial problems may linger for months or even years. It is this "waiting process" that is clearly the most formidable for those I have counseled. They express things like, "I just want it to be over" and "When will my life turn around?" Why, then, doesn't God just fix all of our problems quickly so we don't have to endure the pain? The answer seems to be found in Romans 5:3-6 (NIV) "... but we also rejoice in our sufferings, because we know that suffering produces perseverance; perseverance, character; and character, hope. And hope does not disappoint us, because God has poured out his love into our hearts by the Holy Spirit, whom he has given us."

This text clearly reveals to us that perseverance serves the purpose of building character. Therefore, God's plan for creating our moral and ethical strength is rooted in perseverance. It is during the tough times in our life that we are forced to look upward and to depend on the Lord for our strength. This experience and communion may have never occurred without the accompanying trial that brought us to our knees.

One man I know believes that his marriage was saved by a financial crisis. He explained to me that for years he questioned his wife's true love for him and he even considered divorce. He often wondered if she just loved him for his money. The time came when he lost nearly everything. Instead of leaving him (as he expected), his wife went out to work. She even worked two jobs to help him out of his financial bind. Wow, was he surprised! His wife really did love him, after all.

A new perspective: rather than asking God why, rejoice in the midst of your trial and ask Him what you can learn from this experience. Be open to the lessons that your circumstances may be offering you, and, most importantly, the opportunity for a deepening of your relationship with Him.

> *"It's supposed to be hard. If it wasn't hard, every-one would do it. The hard is what makes it great"* (Tom Hanks character, Jimmy Dugan)
> FROM THE MOVIE, *A LEAGUE OF THEIR OWN.*

PERSERVERANCE - THE HEART OF A CHAMPION

One of my heroes is my son Jim. Jimmy, as we call him, stuttered until he was almost seven years old. He has always been very shy and not the outgoing type. Today, he is a junior in college and is a very confident and successful young man. He graduated from high school with a 4.0 GPA and is a fantastic jazz trumpet player. There was a turning point in his life when everything seemed to come together for him. While in middle school, he began to take a big interest in wrestling. Yes, my wife and I were horrified, but he would sit for hours watching WWE and other wrestling shows on TV.

Once he entered high school he told us that he was going to try out for the wrestling team. He had been involved in sports like baseball and basketball growing up, but wrestling? He was a very skinny kid and my wife and I really wondered if he would even have a chance at making the wrestling team. We were surprised when he came home from school one day to tell us, "I made it. I am on the wrestling team."

I had never seen my son so energized. He was working out seven days a week, drinking protein shakes, and yes starting to build some muscles as well. We heard such positive feedback from the coach at how hard Jim was working, our minds were really changed. This was really turning out to be a very fruitful experience for him.

The season started and many of the matches were away at other schools, so we only saw him wrestle at his home matches. I don't know anything about wrestling, but I do know that one person wins and the other loses. I would pick Jim up at the school late after an away match and ask him how he did. "Dad I lost my match, but the coach said I am really improving." That was a great attitude, I thought, and not everything is about winning, anyway.

I started to get concerned, though, as the season began to go by and Jim was losing nearly all of his matches, but it did not faze him at all. He would tell us how he was improving and was eventually going to start winning. Toward the end of the season, he did end up winning a couple of matches, but he had gone the entire season losing virtually every single match. Amazingly, he was still happy and enthusastic about wrestling and the losses were no big deal to him.

Jim insisted that my wife and I attend the wrestling awards BBQ dinner that was to take place at one of the students homes at the end of the season. My wife and I gathered around with all of the other parents pool-side while the coach begin giving out awards. In each case he would outline the 'wins' and achievments of the wrestler to be recognized and present them with their award. After a handful of awards were presented to the very best wrestlers, the coach said that there was one last award. He said that each year one wrestler was presented with 'The Heart of A Champion' award. This would go to the wrestler that worked the hardest, had the best attitude, and was an example to the rest of the team. He began to describe the recipient. "This boy has only been in our program one year. I have never seen anyone have a better work ethic. His statistics don't show it, but there is no one else on this team that deserves this award but him. In fact, all of the wrestlers got together and came to me last week and insisted that he receive this award."

My son's name was called out - I was so proud, even prouder than I would have been if he had won the state championship. This is what God wants for us! He wants us to have the heart of a champion and sometimes that means we have to endure some challenges for long periods of time before we see relief.

THE MIRACLE OF A SUMMER BASKETBALL LEAGUE

About two years into my financial collapse, the summer was approaching and my wife had planned to get Jimmy signed up for the local Police Athletic League basketball program. Basketball was his passion before he got the wrestling bug. We went down to the PAL office to sign him up and they said he might not be able to play. The lady explained that due to a lack of coaches they may have to shut down registration early and limit the number of players. I asked her what the qualifications were to coach. She said, "Are you volunteering?" What was I about to get myself into? Other than watching the NBA, I had no basketball experience, either as a player or a coach. Within five minutes I was now the coach of my son's basketball team.

I have to honestly share with you that my self esteem could not have been lower at that time. I felt like a complete loser and the last thing I wanted to do was to take on something I was convinced I would end up failing at, and possibly embarrass my son at in the process. What was done was done. I was told to show up at the recreation center the following week for the 'draft.' The gym was filled with kids that would each dribble the ball up and shoot a jump shot and a lay up. From that, we were supposed to begin the process of choosing the players in a round robin fashion in an adjoining meeting room.

I was already at a huge disadvantage being new to all of this. The other coaches had coached for years and were very familiar with the pool of kids we were going to be picking from. Each coach's name was put into a hat and the order they were drawn out would establish the order we would pick in. My name came out of the hat last. There was one positive in that, however, which is that I would get the first pick in the second round. Nonetheless, I knew I was in trouble and missed out on the star players that were all taken before my turn. Knowing absolutely nothing, I thought I would go for the better ball handlers as the tallest players were already taken. I drafted my ten players and began my adventure into basketball coaching.

In preparation, I went down to our local library and checked out a dozen or so books and a couple of videos on how to coach basketball. I was actually starting to enjoy this. I ran several drills from the book in our first practice and made it our focus that we were going to be a passing and running team, making up in agility what we did not have in height.

The first game came and I was scared to death about what would happen. I had to pick my starters and establish a bench rotation. This was all completely terrifying to me (and it looked a lot easier when I watched it on TV). My wife was trying to be encouraging, but I think she, too, was nervous for me, knowing how brittle my self esteem was. No one was more shocked than I when we won our first game.

The season progressed and we continued to win game after game. I just could not believe it! At the end of the season we were nine wins and no losses and just one game to go. We won our final game and went undefeated. 10-0 it was a perfect season! I remember a lady and a man from the recreation office coming out on to the floor and awarding each of my kids their first place trophy. I could simply not comprehend how we went undefeated, but I knew that this was a special gift from the Lord to me, His way of saying, "You may be down now, but you are not out. You still have a lot to offer and this is just the start." That winning season still sticks out in my memory as a real turning point in my recovery.

ARE WE THERE YET?

If you have ever taken a driving vacation with your children, you have no doubt heard the question, "Are we there yet?" a few thousand times. Sometimes God's answer is not *no*, but *not now*. Some trials are longer than others, and these are character building opportunities for us. Easy to write in a book, but not so easy to live out in real life.

I remember one well-meaning relative that would regularly call me to ask how I was doing. I would start sharing all of the issues I was going through and they would say, "Just move forward with your life, stop looking in the past." What they didn't understand was that I would have loved to do just that, but the process of settling all of the legal issues involved in my financial collapse was a full time job for three years and a part time job for two years beyond that. My bankruptcy took two and a half years to complete, since millions of dollars were involved in what was deemed a 'complex bankruptcy.' To make matters worse, I could not afford an attorney to handle my bankruptcy. I spent so much time in court and preparing for court, that it was all I could do to just keep my bankruptcy case going. I truly believe that God was building a heart of a champion in me during those years. At the time, I would never have accepted that, but now I can see it as clearly as ever and I believe that God was fulfilling Romans 8:28 and Romans 5:3-4 in my life.

GETTING FOCUSED GETS RESULTS

One of the things we know is that when a person focuses on a single problem they can usually solve it, sometimes even without prayer. Imagine how much more we can accomplish with God's help! Consider the example of Dave Ramsey, known for his strategies on paying off debt, who has been at odds with many financial teachers on the foundation of his methodology. Ramsey suggests that his students start their debt reduction plan by taking their smallest debt and paying all of their extra money toward it until it is paid off (his so called 'snowball' method). After that, take the next smallest, and so on. Critics have said that this is not the most financially efficient method and have suggested that starting with the debt that has the highest interest rate would make more sense. A study published in the August 2012 edition of the Journal of Marketing Research vindicated Ramsey. The study of 4,200 consumers provided empirical evidence that the idea of focusing all of your efforts on the smallest debt first produced the best results. The reason why Ramsey's 'system' works is that when we focus our energy like a laser beam on a single bite-sized problem, we usually solve it. Rather than seeing a mountain of debt, Ramsey's students see one debt at a time. It is a real confidence builder to start paying off the small obligations first, which is why his method is so successful.

TAKE TIME TO THINK THROUGH YOUR PROBLEMS

Former president Harry Truman said his years as a Missouri farmer and long days riding the plow gave him time to think and form his own opinions. Truman was quoted as saying, "The most peaceful thing in the world is plowing a field. Chances are you'll do your best thinking that way. And that's why I've always thought and said, farmers are the smartest people in the world, they don't go for high hats and they can spot a phony a mile off."

WHAT ABOUT PRAYING FOR A BAG OF MONEY?

At ChristianMoney.com, we receive quite a large volume of e mail from people looking for answers to a myriad of financial crises they are facing. Many of them are focused on what I call 'the bag of money prayer.' I need $1,000 by Friday or else (you fill in the blank). These kinds of prayers are answered, and just as in the story of my own family, God can and does meet our financial needs in more ways than I can count. I am reminded of Luke 11:11 -13 (NIV) "Which of you fathers, if your son asks for a fish, will give him a snake instead? Or if he asks for an egg, will give him a scorpion? If you then, though you are evil, know how to give good gifts to your children, how much more will your Father in heaven give the Holy Spirit to those who ask him!"

I believe that there is a very deep and significant meaning in this passage. The Lord is saying here that He will give us good gifts and provide what is best for us. I think it is in many ways a much more complete gift from the Lord to receive wisdom than a bag of money. Wisdom is not just an answer for today's problem but the know how of avoiding the pitfalls that got us here in the first place. We also know from the countless stories of lottery winners, that windfalls of money are not necessarily a blessing. All too often, receiving large sums of money can be the source of major strife.

APPROACHING GOD LIKE HE IS A GENIE ABOUT TO GRANT THREE WISHES

There are some people that view God much like the idea of a genie. One of my favorite episodes in the Three Stooges TV show was when Curly found an old genie's lamp. He said, "Moe, let's rub it and see if there is a genius inside." There are some denominations that approach God with the idea that if they quote the right verse or speak a series of special words that He must give them what they are asking for. The Lord loves us too much to answer our prays this way. Just as a parent, He knows what is in our best interest and what gifts will serve the ultimate purpose of making us more like Him.

ASKING OTHERS TO PRAY FOR YOU

Again, this is going to fall into the category of something I don't completely understand but know it to be true in my own life and biblical. God does hear and answer our prayers, even if we are the only one praying. There is, however, a powerful synergy that occurs when multitudes of people are praying for someone. **Matthew 18:20 (KJV) "For where two or three are gathered together in my name, there am I in the midst of them."** Why do we have prayer chains and prayer requests in church, why not just keep our problems and prayers to ourselves? There have been countless books written on the concept of intercessory prayer. Prayer is a *group* activity, share your needs with your fellow Christians and ask for their prayers.

SEEKING GUIDANCE AND WISE COUNSEL

There are times when you will not be able to see the solution to your financial challenge and your answer will come by way of a godly person whose counsel you seek. **Proverbs 15:22 (NIV) "Plans fail for lack of counsel, but with many advisers they succeed."** There are so many people around you right now that not only want to help, but that God has specially equipped to help you in your exact situation.

One of the blessings that has come out of my own personal financial collapse is the ability to empathize with those that are going through the same circumstances. It is very hard to relate with someone in their trial unless you have been there yourself. One of the real tragedies of many churches today is that people don't share their problems. This creates an illusion for the struggling individual that he is the only one and that everyone else has a perfect life. This has been further propagated by social media. Most of us only post to our social media accounts the good things going on in our lives.

Recently a friend was sharing with me how deeply depressed he was about his financial situation. He went on Facebook and started reviewing his newsfeed, and it seemed like everyone in his circle of friends and relatives was doing wonderful. One of his friends posted a picture of her and her husband with a beautiful tan on a Florida beach. The post went on to share what a wonderful time they were having on their two week vacation. I happen to know this couple myself and reminded my friend of the multiple tragedies this family faced in recent years, including cancer and the death of two close family members. Life is cyclical and we will all have seasons of prosperity and seasons when we are struggling. Don't add to your stress by believing a lie from the enemy that you are the only one facing adversity.

CHAPTER SIX

Thinking Outside The Box

As a money manager, I used to review my stock positions daily and simply ask myself if I would buy these stocks again today if they were not already in my portfolio. This was a very good discipline and was an intellectually honest way to keep myself from holding on to investments that should be sold. In many ways, we do this in our own lives. The major justification we have for staying on our current course is that it is how we have always done things. It is amazing how shallow this approach is and yet we all have done it. Maybe we believe that keeping things just as they are is the path of least resistance, but that may not really be the case. Who knows if there is not a better way than the current path we are on?

JOINT VENTURING WITH GOD

Implicit in many prayers is the notion that it is up to God to act, and I simply sit back and wait as the recipient for Him to deliver what I need. The reality is, and we see so many examples of this in Scripture, that many problems are answered through a *joint venture with God*. We pray and ask for His blessing, but at the same time work to do everything we can on our own. There's an old saying, "Pray as if it all depends on God and work as if it all depends on you." This quote has been attributed to Ignatius but there is no real evidence that he said it. I do like this concept very much and find no conflict in the idea that a financial miracle can be the product of God's blessings and my best efforts combined.

As the Editor-In-Chief of ChristianMoney.com, I write several articles per month focusing primarily on ways to save money and ways to earn money. I am constantly on the prowl, looking for little-known methods of saving money and also some quite unusual and unique ideas on making money. At the heart of most financial crises is a financial shortfall. That is, there is more outflow than inflow of money.

For example, a $2,000 monthly mortgage payment may represent a 'crisis' for someone that is only earning $3,000 per month, but may be just fine for an individual earning $7,500 monthly. What we can conclude from this simple example is that the mortgage, in and of itself, is not the crisis. It is the amount of the mortgage within the context of an individual's monthly income.

CONSIDERING SOMETHING CRAZY, LIKE MOVING ACROSS THE COUNTRY, OR EVEN ACROSS THE GLOBE

One of my wife's favorite TV shows to watch is House Hunters. The reality show lets you tag along and watch as prospective home buyers tour homes and decide which one they will purchase. The episodes she enjoys most are the ones that involve house hunting outside the United States. It is really fascinating to see how many places that a person can live a genuinely wonderful lifestyle for a fraction of the cost of living in the U.S. Ann and I have discussed on many occasions maybe selling everything and moving to a foreign country and living out our retirement years abroad.

I am always looking for lists on the cheapest places to live, and as much as I follow the topic, I am always surprised at what I discover. One website I love to look at is Realtor.com. You can type in any city, your criteria for number of bedrooms and bathrooms, and instantly get a price list of what is available. For example, at the time of writing this book there are pages of listings of four bedroom homes for less than $50,000 in Las Vegas. I am not suggesting that you or I move to Las Vegas necessarily, but I want to use this to illustrate a very important point.

I regularly receive e mails from people that are in such desperate situations financially that they are literally sick. One man, several years ago, called in to my radio show to tell us that he had a gun and was going to kill himself. We contacted the police in San Francisco and they were able to locate him and stop him; thank God. I was there myself during my financial crisis, perceiving that my life was over and considering suicide. While you may not be there yourself, it is a very slippery slope and don't kid yourself that you could never get to a low point such as this.

There are so many people today in the depths of despair mostly due to the high price of housing where they live. Imagine being able to buy a home for just $50,000 and how much easier your life would be. Las Vegas is just one example of a city where it easy to find low cost housing. of course, I realize that there are other factors such as employment opportunities that must be considered as well. This is one of the reasons I am so enthusiastic about working online as it allows you true geographic freedom and you can live anywhere you can connect to the Internet. I made reference earlier in this book to Steubenville, Ohio, which has 100 percent employment due to the area's oil and gas boom. Can you believe that a few months ago when I wrote an article on this city, typical monthly rent for a home was only $500!

GETTING OUT OF THE MUD AND
FINDING A NEW PERSPECTIVE

As I mentioned previously, my wife convinced me to go to counseling and there is no doubt that it saved my life. My counselor, Dr. Rafael Parlade (to whom this book is dedicated), taught me so many very valuable lessons. The one major lesson that I want to share with you in this chapter is that you choose what meaning to assign to the events in your life. This is literally the most powerful and freeing concept that I have ever learned. It was a game changer for me, and if you are right now in the depths of financial despair, it can be a breakthrough moment for you as well.

Each of my counseling appointments lasted about 45 minutes. My sessions would always start with Dr. Parlade asking me how I was doing. I loved having someone like this to talk to and would plan out a day or two in advance of my session what topics I was going to bring up. The real benefit of counseling for me was that I could share anything that was on my mind without having to be concerned about how it might sound, or being judged. I would usually start with a couple of items of good news. Typically, issues I had brought up in prior counseling sessions that had come to a resolution. Next, I would transition into a list of my current struggles (and there were many). He would hear me out and then ask how each situation made me feel. I would honestly share my feelings, most of which could be described as feeling like a complete failure.

"OK, you are filing for bankruptcy because you were the victim of an embezzlement scheme, right?" he would ask. I would go on to share how absolutely humiliating it was to be going bankrupt as a financial expert, author, and speaker. He would point out that a lot of people have gone through bankruptcy and it is not a defining moment, it is just an event. "You will get through this and be an even more insightful financial writer when this is all over." Wow, could he be right? Could the meaning I have attached to this situation be completely wrong? Was it possible that there could be some positive that could come out of all of this?

One thing was for sure, I was going bankrupt and I had no choice or control over that. I did, however, have a choice as to the meaning that I gave to it. This was so empowering! My life was completely spiraling out of control and I found something that I actually had control over. Instead of instinctively believing that bankruptcy equals failure, I could instead see my bankruptcy as an opportunity.

I began to think about how badly I was beating myself up for years about all of this. This was not God's plan and Dr. Parlade was 100% right. In each counseling session he would find numerous things to compliment me and encourage me about. During one session, I was sharing with him all of the long and tiring stages of my bankruptcy. I remember one especially low point when the bankruptcy trustee sent an appraiser to our rented home. When you file for bankruptcy, you are required to list all of your assets. In my own case, the appraiser came out for about an hour to our home. I made sure to schedule this during the day when I would be the only one home.

The appraiser was an older lady and she was very nice. She asked me how I ended up in bankruptcy and was just as fascinated with the story of the embezzlement as everyone else. I took her through every room of the house, and she had the list of assets I had listed in the bankruptcy. As I showed her the kids rooms she explained that the children's toys and clothes were not going to be counted as part of my bankruptcy estate. I had a piano and a grandfather clock that I had inherited years earlier from my grandparents. Other than my trumpet, these were the only items that really seemed to represent any value. I guess losing everything made her review of my assets a pretty simple project.

Parlade sat listening as I shared the details about the bankruptcy appraiser coming to the house. I told him how humiliated I was. I even had to show them my children's rooms, toys, they went through my closet, even my underwear drawer. He said, "Look you have a lot to feel good about in all of this. How many people could go to federal bankruptcy court and represent themselves without an attorney? The appraiser coming out to your house just means that you are all that much closer to the bankruptcy being over and then you can move on with your life."

Parlade was simply a master at turning my failures into successes. It was like I was a pitcher throwing the most awful pitches in the dirt and he would find a way to hit home runs with them. What's more, he was right! He was not just feeding me pyscho-babble, I did have a lot to be proud of. Without being an attorney I was able to go into court and handle a multi-million dollar bankruptcy. I was proud to share with him that on two occasions the bankruptcy judge, by mistake, referred to me as an attorney representing myself. I corrected the judge, but on one occasion he said, "Mr. Paris you must have an attorney. If you are not an attorney, how are you completing these legal filings?" I explained that I had spent a lot of time in the local law library and was self taught. He looked at me in disbelief, shook his head, and moved on.

CHOOSING TO SEE YOUR CIRCUMSTANCES IN A POSITIVE LIGHT

There is always an opportunity to find a 'glass is half full' perspective if you look for it. What I wanted every single day of those five years, was to just have it all over. I saw no virtue in taking years to get out of my financial quagmire. Along the way, there were so many 'glass is half full' moments, I am still just realizing some of them while organizing my thoughts to write this book.

You don't have to be a Pollyanna and ignore the pain that you might be in right now. Your financial miracle may very well be over the next horizon and in order to see it you must be able to lift your eyes, if even just for a moment.

There were so many occasions when I looked at my life and it appeared to be nothing more than shattered hopes and dreams. I believed that my life was so irreparably damaged that there would be no way that God could ever use me again. I can honestly tell you that if it was all for the sole purpose of being able to have this story to share, my testimony of an amazing and dark journey that ended with renewed hope for an even brighter future – it was worth it.

CHAPTER SEVEN

Living Out My Financial Miracle

Today, I am a changed person from who I was before my financial collapse. My focus now is finding out what the Lord is doing and joining Him in His work, rather than running ahead and expecting Him to bless my own plans.

One of the lessons that came out of the embezzlement was that I would not run any business or enterprise that was larger than I could personally monitor every element of. For now, that means I work from a home office and between my partner and I we do most of the writing for ChristianMoney.com. We hire several independent contractors that also work from their homes doing computer programming, website design, and other tasks that we delegate. Some may view this 'downsized' version of Jim Paris as a disappointment comparing to my prior multiple corporate holdings and dozens of employees. I honestly believe that in my current configuration I am able to reach just as many people and make just as big a difference, notwithstanding having just a fraction of my prior infrastructure.

My ability to leverage myself comes mostly from the advancement in technology. I can now produce my own Internet radio show in a home office completely on my own. We are able to publish our own books and e Books, just like this one you are reading now (which is a completely self published work). Through the Internet, we are able to get our articles and videos distributed worldwide for pennies on the dollar compared to what distribution would have cost just ten years ago. I guess some might say reading this, "You picked a great time to reinvent yourself." I could not agree more with this and I invite you to join me.

One of the issues that comes to my doorstep each day is people facing a lack of income. I know that there are some very fine organizations that have tremendous resources for Christians on the topic of budgeting and learning to live within one's means. The organizations I would recommend for this kind of help would include Dave Ramsey and Crown Financial Ministries. I have felt that the part of the problem that I am called to address is that of helping Christians to create additional income.

After my bankruptcy, the only thing left was my website. The problem was that I had never tried to make money directly from the website itself. I always viewed it as sort of an online brochure with the idea that its role was to promote the other things I was doing. For example, the website was used heavily to promote my financial planning business, books I would write, speaking engagements, and my radio and TV programs. Once I was down to nothing but the website, I had to convert it from an advertising tool to an income generating asset.

In the beginning, figuring out how to make money directly from my website was not easy. You have to keep in mind that this was more than ten years ago and the idea of making money online as a solo entrepreneur was not even in its infancy. I began to learn about what today we call 'monetization.' That is, how to create an online presence, drive visitors to it, and then convert all of that into a stream of money.

It took me a good five years to reach the point that I really knew what I was doing. About five years ago I was asked to guest host the nationally syndicated Point of View Radio show. The topic we agreed to center the discussion on was estate planning. We were offering one of my estate planning books to listeners that made a gift to support their ministry. Just a few minutes into the first day of my two days of hosting, a caller brought up the subject of how to make money online with a website. You can imagine, that was like setting a ball on a tee and giving me a fat bat. I began to share my own experiences and methods that I was using to make my full time living using the Internet.

After this first question was called in, it led to a second, and the program I was supposed to be hosting on the topic of estate planning became all about *making money online*. Point of View immediately scheduled me for several additional appearances that would all focus on Internet business.

It was just after the radio broadcasts on Point of View that Daystar TV called and asked me to appear during their live spring fundraising broadcast. We would offer the viewers a package of materials on how to start an Internet business. The rest, as they say, is history. My day is focused on two major business activities: First, the care and feeding of my own Internet business, and secondly, on developing materials and training designed to teach others how to do what I am doing.

For me, the Internet provides the ultimate in flexibility. I get to make my own hours and decide what location I work from. All I need is an Internet connection and I can 'go to work.' Working from home or my small sailboat is probably the best part of being an Internet entrepreneur. I love people and enjoy my opportunities of speaking to large groups, but I also really love my simple life in Palm Coast, FL. Many times I ditch my car for the day and just cruise around on my 150cc scooter. I wear a small backpack that I use to carry my laptop computer with me. With a wireless card I pay $50 monthly for, I don't even need a wifi hotspot. I can, and regularly do, simply find a nice spot at the beach and pull out my laptop and begin working.

The other fantastic benefit of working online is the ability to build a residual income. Over the years, I have written hundreds of articles and filmed dozens of videos. Each time I write an article or produce a video, I can post it online and then sit back and earn money from that one day's work for years and years. I have one video right now on YouTube that I earn about $15 a day from. Just that one video! If you want to check out my YouTube Channel, my username is jameslparis.

I have been trying desperately to get the information out on what I am doing to as many people as possible, especially God's people. I currently offer several free online workshops each week that are designed to shed light on the large variety of different ways there are to earn money from the Internet. I don't believe that every one of these opportunities is right for everyone, which is why I offer such a variety of choices.

I have some students that want to set up a simple website on a topic that they have an interest in. They want to learn how to build and maintain the site and how to create a daily income from it. I have other students that have taken off like a rocket on the whole opportunity of e Books (probably my favorite one). Other students love the idea of producing videos and posting them to YouTube as a means of generating an income. One Christian family that goes by the name "The Shaytards" on YouTube, produces the most hilarious videos. In essence, they have created their own reality show that they broadcast through a channel on YouTube. The money they earn from their videos represents their full time income. They appeared on Dave Ramsey's show to share how they were able to pay off all of their debts with the money earned with their YouTube channel! I just love to hear stories like this.

The reasons that people want to pursue an online business are as varied as the number of people I hear from. Some want to build up an online business as a means to being able to quit their 'day job.' Others simply want to cultivate a part time business and use the proceeds to build up their savings, pay down their debts, and have a few extra bucks for gas, groceries, and the kids. There is nothing wrong with this approach, either. Still others are building online businesses as their retirement plan.

Due to the residual income that can be generated from an online business, it represents an excellent retirement strategy. The work that you do today can produce an income for years, maybe even decades. There is so much wealth being created through online businesses today, that it has become a hot topic within estate planning circles. It is no longer a matter of who wants my house when I die, but who wants my website (and the daily income it is generating). Lawyers and financial planners in recent years have had to go back to school to learn how to handle the distribution of 'virtual' assets in wills and trusts.

If you are interested in learning more about starting your own online business, check out one of my upcoming free workshops. You will find the schedule and registration links at *www.jimsfreetraining.com*.

OTHER WEBSITES OF MINE:

www.ChristianMoney.com

www.MakeMoneyWithAWebsite.US

www.MakeMoneyWithAnEbook.us

James Paris
138 Palm Coast Parkway NE, #223
Palm Coast, FL 32137

JIM PARIS MONTHLY NEWSLETTER

Bob Yetman and I produce a twelve page monthly newsletter that has become quite unique in its content. We started out in the beginning with two separate newsletters. One newsletter covered topics related to making money online and the other was on Bible prophecy and survival. We have combined these two newsletters into one and you can have it mailed to your home each month for $9.95. After the cost of producing and mailing the newsletter, the balance of the proceeds are used to help us to continue to fulfill our mission of bringing this information to the Christian community. Subscriptions orders can be placed online at *www.jimparisnewsletter.com*.

HOW TO PRAY FOR A FINANCIAL MIRACLE ONLINE COMMUNITY

Please take a minute and join our online community at *www.financialmiraclebook.com*. This site will serve as the home base for announcements of my media appearances and speaking engagements on this book. We also are excited to be making available an interactive forum where you can post your own prayer requests and pray for others' needs, as well.

CHAPTER EIGHT

The Financial Miracle Prayer

1. Thank the Lord for all of your blessings. Take ample time to really consider all that He has already done for you.

2. Ask Him to reveal what you may have done to contribute to the financial challenge you are now facing and ask for His forgiveness.

3. Pray about one financial challenge at a time. Ask Him for wisdom to develop a plan of action.

4. **Very Important:** Begin to list the ideas and solutions that come to mind as you remain in a state of reverence and prayer. The following pages are already set up for this purpose. Do not rush this process. The Lord will speak to you.

5. Ask Him to lead you to individuals that may be worthy counselors for this issue.

6.   Ask Him to bless your best efforts in acting on the ideas and solutions He has provided.

7.   Thank the Lord again, and accept His will for your life on the outcome of this financial challenge.

8.   Don't limit God. He can meet your needs in so many ways you can't even imagine right now.

9.   Share your need with God's people and ask them to pray with you.

10.   Have faith and expect a financial miracle!

11.   Pray repeatedly about this issue as the status changes over time.

Today's Date:_____

Financial Issue You Are Praying About:

_____

_____

_____

_____

_____

_____

_____

_____

_____

_____

_____

_____

_____

Ideas and Solutions:

_____

_____

_____

_____

_____

_____

_____

_____

_____

_____

_____

_____

_____

Today's Date:_____

Financial Issue You Are Praying About:

_____

_____

_____

_____

_____

_____

_____

_____

_____

_____

_____

_____

_____

Ideas and Solutions:

_____

_____

_____

_____

_____

_____

_____

_____

_____

_____

_____

_____

_____

_____

Today's Date:_____

Financial Issue You Are Praying About:

_____

_____

_____

_____

_____

_____

_____

_____

_____

_____

_____

_____

_____

Ideas and Solutions:

_____

_____

_____

_____

_____

_____

_____

_____

_____

_____

_____

_____

_____

_____

Today's Date:＿＿＿＿＿＿＿＿＿＿＿＿＿＿＿＿

Financial Issue You Are Praying About:

＿＿＿＿＿＿＿＿＿＿＿＿＿＿＿＿＿＿＿＿＿

＿＿＿＿＿＿＿＿＿＿＿＿＿＿＿＿＿＿＿＿＿

＿＿＿＿＿＿＿＿＿＿＿＿＿＿＿＿＿＿＿＿＿

＿＿＿＿＿＿＿＿＿＿＿＿＿＿＿＿＿＿＿＿＿

＿＿＿＿＿＿＿＿＿＿＿＿＿＿＿＿＿＿＿＿＿

＿＿＿＿＿＿＿＿＿＿＿＿＿＿＿＿＿＿＿＿＿

＿＿＿＿＿＿＿＿＿＿＿＿＿＿＿＿＿＿＿＿＿

＿＿＿＿＿＿＿＿＿＿＿＿＿＿＿＿＿＿＿＿＿

＿＿＿＿＿＿＿＿＿＿＿＿＿＿＿＿＿＿＿＿＿

＿＿＿＿＿＿＿＿＿＿＿＿＿＿＿＿＿＿＿＿＿

＿＿＿＿＿＿＿＿＿＿＿＿＿＿＿＿＿＿＿＿＿

＿＿＿＿＿＿＿＿＿＿＿＿＿＿＿＿＿＿＿＿＿

＿＿＿＿＿＿＿＿＿＿＿＿＿＿＿＿＿＿＿＿＿

Ideas and Solutions:

_____

_____

_____

_____

_____

_____

_____

_____

_____

_____

_____

_____

_____

_____

Today's Date:_____

Financial Issue You Are Praying About:

_____

_____

_____

_____

_____

_____

_____

_____

_____

_____

_____

_____

_____

Ideas and Solutions:

_____

_____

_____

_____

_____

_____

_____

_____

_____

_____

_____

_____

_____

_____

Today's Date:_____

Financial Issue You Are Praying About:

_____

_____

_____

_____

_____

_____

_____

_____

_____

_____

_____

_____

_____

Ideas and Solutions:

Today's Date:_____

Financial Issue You Are Praying About:

_____

_____

_____

_____

_____

_____

_____

_____

_____

_____

_____

_____

_____

Ideas and Solutions:

_____

_____

_____

_____

_____

_____

_____

_____

_____

_____

_____

_____

_____

Today's Date:_____

Financial Issue You Are Praying About:

_____

_____

_____

_____

_____

_____

_____

_____

_____

_____

_____

_____

_____

Ideas and Solutions:

_____

_____

_____

_____

_____

_____

_____

_____

_____

_____

_____

_____

_____

_____

Today's Date:_____

Financial Issue You Are Praying About:

_____

_____

_____

_____

_____

_____

_____

_____

_____

_____

_____

_____

_____

Ideas and Solutions:

_____

_____

_____

_____

_____

_____

_____

_____

_____

_____

_____

_____

_____

_____

Today's Date:_____

Financial Issue You Are Praying About:

_____

_____

_____

_____

_____

_____

_____

_____

_____

_____

_____

_____

_____

Ideas and Solutions:

APPENDIX I

How To Become A Christian

I expect this book to have a very large worldwide distribution. The Lord has impressed upon my heart the importance of sharing how to become one of His followers with you. If you have never accepted the Lord into your heart as your personal savior, please consider doing so today. This is not about joining a church or a denomination, but beginning a real relationship with the God of the universe.

You can become a follower of Christ and receive salvation and eternal life by simply praying the following prayer:

Dear Jesus:
I want to have a relationship with you. I know I can't save myself, because I know I'm a sinner. Thank you for dying on the cross on my behalf. I believe you died for me, and I accept your free gift of salvation.

Thank you Jesus.

Amen.

You can pray this prayer right now, where you are. It does not matter if you are reading this book on an airplane, if you are sitting in a coffee shop, or relaxing on a sofa at home. After you have prayed this prayer, I would recommend that you read the book of John in the New Testament and find a local bible believing church to become involved with in your city. I would also recommend visiting the *Reasoning From The Scriptures* website and their excellent outline on *How To Become A Christian*.

If you have made a decision today to follow Christ as your savior, I would love to hear from you. Please share the wonderful news with me Jim@ChristianMoney.com.

APPENDIX II

Photos

Jim Paris and family October 29, 2012

Gratitude

Six-year-old Jimmy Park, a patient in Community hospital, wanted to say thank you to all the nurses who have him such tender loving care while he was there. The gratitude came in the form of a cake with Charlie Brown characters taking on the roles of doctor, nurse and patient. Before cutting and serving the special treat to all the nurses and patients, Jimmy and Head Nurse Mrs. Mathke-Durakowilez R.N. took time out for a sample. Jimmy is now at home with his parents at 9130 S. Odell, Bridgeview.

Newspaper story from 1971 from Jim's first childhood accident. Jim is sharing a cake with the nurses made by Bobbi Bestwina, one of his neighbors from Odell Avenue in Bridgeview.

Jim With Pat Robertson after one of more than 25 appearances on The 700 Club

Jim's 2002 summer basketball team

Ann and Jim Paris married November 10, 1986

2 Guys With Horns. Jim and Paul Ricci performing at an antique car show in Daytona Beach.

ACKNOWLEDGEMENTS

My wonderful family. My wife Ann, and children Joy, Jimmy, and Faith. Thanks for standing by me during the tough times.

My mother Sharon Paris and my sister Becky Roberts for always being there for me.

Dad, I miss you - hope you are looking down and proud of me.

The Christian media outlets that supported us during our darkest hours. Including Moody Radio Network – Mark Elfstrand, Dave Mitchell, Brian Dahlen and crew. Christian Television Network– Herman and Sharron Bailey. Point of View Radio- Marlin and Mary Maddoux, Kerby Anderson, and Warren Kelley. Daystar TV- Marcus and Joni Lamb.

My pastors over the last decade, Larry Kirk, Dennis Kiggins, David Posey, and Jamie Sellers. Thanks for your love and support.

My business partner Bob Yetman and his wife Dallas. We have had a lot of great memories and our best days are still ahead.

Pastor Kevin Craig of Apopka Assembly, and Mark Anthony of Bread of Life Fellowship. Both of these men continue to support my parent's dream and mission of feeding the needy through the Storehouse Ministry of Apopka Assembly of God.

My former publisher for many years, Harvest House Publishers. Bob Hawkins, Jr. and Bob Hawkins, Sr. have been wonderful friends to our organization over the years. During my financial collapse they continued to work with me, promoted my books, and those royalty checks were a real lifesaver.